KILIMANJARO

ONE MAN'S QUEST TO GO OVER THE HILL

M.G. EDWARDS

BRILLIANCE PRESS
2012

For information about permission to reproduce selections from this
book, contact:

Brilliance Press
14781 Memorial Dr., Suite #1392
Houston, TX 77079
Visit our website at www.mgedwards.com

First Paperback Edition: April 2012

Edwards, Michael, 1970 —
Kilimanjaro: One Man's Quest to Go Over the Hill / by M.G.
Edwards. — 1st ed.
p. cm.
Summary: The author attempts to summit Mount Kilimanjaro, the highest
mountain in Africa, to overcome a mid-life crisis and change his life.

ISBN: 978-1-470-16198-9 (Paperback)

Printed in the United States of America

For my wife, Jing
The best climber in our family

ᔆ ᔄ

For my husband, who
sometimes drives me
around the bend, but
will never be "over the hill"
Good luck + Merry
                    Christmas
                        2012
        Love you so much
                    Me x
                    x x x x
                        x x x

CONTENTS

Maps of Kilimanjaro Routes

Major Kilimanjaro Climbing Routes

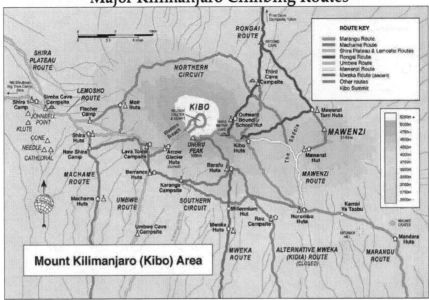

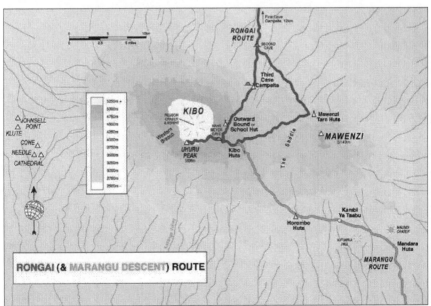

Maps from "Kilimanjaro – A Trekking Guide to Africa's Highest Mountain" by Henry Stedman. Trailblazer Publications; 3rd edition. Courtesy of Henry Stedman.

1. Facing My Mountains

I sat in the medical clinic desperate for a quick cure of my ailment. I was days away from departing for the climb of my life, and I felt miserable. I was in questionable condition to attempt to summit Mount Kilimanjaro, Africa's tallest mountain. My chest tightened, and I had trouble drawing deep breaths. My nose was stuffed up, and I was nauseated. I had no idea what I had. I fought my undiagnosed respiratory problem with a variety of inhalers, antibiotics and other medications, but nothing brought me back to health. Everything from a severe flu to tuberculosis crossed my mind, but the medics eliminated more possibilities with each visit to the clinic. As I sat in her office, the nurse suggested that I had severe allergies. She asked, "Are you sure you want to do the climb? You might have a difficult time breathing. Things may get worse the higher you go."

I thought through my response. I could not make it to the top of Kilimanjaro if I couldn't breathe. My mind told me to defer my climb until I felt better, but my heart refused. I pushed aside my misgivings and decided to go ahead with it. I felt better than I had the previous week, I reasoned, and would be recovered enough to climb before I traveled. After a brief pause, I told her, "Yes, I do. I'm feeling much better. Really."

She looked skeptical but could see that I was determined to go ahead with my adventure. "Okay, then take a combination of the inhalers, and use this one if you feel tightness in your chest. If your condition gets any worse before you go, call me right away."

"I will," I said. I was relieved that I had the remedy I needed to get through my respiratory problem. I did not want to attempt Mount Kilimanjaro without some reassurance that I could handle the high altitude, low oxygen levels, and strenuous trek to 5,895 meters (19,341 feet) above sea level in my current condition. With one week left before the biggest challenge of my life, my mind was the only part of my body prepared for it. I left the clinic with inhalers and medications in hand, debating whether to climb. One by one, I dismissed my reservations with each footfall on the pavement.

I had never been seriously ill until I moved in 2009 to Zambia, a country in southern Africa with its fair share of pandemics, from malaria to cholera. Soon after I arrived at my new home in Lusaka, I developed severe allergies and high blood pressure, and put on a lot of weight. My health deteriorated precipitously, sapping my strength.

My wife, Jing, who was always my voice of reason, cautioned me not to attempt Kilimanjaro if I wasn't ready for it. Several times she asked me with concern in her voice, "Are you sure you want to do it when you're sick?"

"Yes, I'm sure," I answered her every time. "I need to do it...for me."

"Then why not postpone your trip?" she asked. Jing had reason to be worried. She summited Mount Kilimanjaro the year before and knew how difficult it was. Her suggestion was logical, but I had already invested too much in this endeavor. The trip had been months in planning, and I had gone to great lengths to get in shape for it in spite of my respiratory issues. After a brief pause, I said, "No, I can't, hon. I need to get better and climb this mountain."

She shook her head. "Okay, but think about it."

The future weighed on my mind. Approaching middle age, I was overweight and out of shape, living a sedentary lifestyle, and stuck in a rut. A series of personal setbacks left me a bitter man. Every time I was convinced life would get better, another letdown hit me. A midlife crisis, something that just a few years ago I never thought possible, was brewing.

After Jing returned from Kilimanjaro, I decided that I needed to do it too. A physical challenge greater than any I had ever faced, scaling Africa's highest peak was just what I needed to jumpstart my life at middle age. I was certain it would test my mettle and prepare me for whatever obstacles the future threw at me. Making it over this mountain would help me get over the hill.

Climbing Kilimanjaro was a prelude to leaving my job as an American diplomat. I had a career that many people admired and a comfortable lifestyle that allowed me to travel to exotic places and have amazing experiences, and yet, I was unhappy. I found the diplomatic life frustrating. The Foreign Service offered some glorious moments, but it also meant bending to the will of the U.S. Government, conforming to a byzantine bureaucracy, and fighting for survival in a stifling work environment, an atmosphere that left me cold as a climber freezing in a frosty bivouac. I had enough and decided to resign to follow my true passion, writing. I debated and second-guessed myself for months, wondering why I would leave a stable job for an untested career. I had not yet submitted my letter of resignation and decided to use my time on the climb to think about my decision.

I did not want to end up like Harry Street, the washed-up character in Ernest Hemingway's 1936 short story *The Snows of Kilimanjaro*, who spent his final days dying from an infected wound in the shadow of Mount Kilimanjaro. Harry lamented over his failed life and the ambitions he never fulfilled because he gave in to his own weaknesses. Shattered dreams tormented him until his untimely death. His soul floated away to the icy heights of Kilimanjaro, his body left behind in the visage of a frozen leopard carcass lying in the snow. I wasn't about to suffer the same fate as

Harry, a man who lived a life of unfulfilled aspirations. Walking away from the climb — a challenge that would help me get past my midlife crisis and into my later years — was not an option. I needed to find my passion again and to pursue what I wanted to do since I was young — be a writer. At middle age, my life was half over, and I didn't want to spend the rest of my days regretting my past like Harry did.

Leaving the medical clinic, I wondered whether I had the resolve and fortitude to reach the summit of Kilimanjaro, quit my job, and get my life back. In the midst of a midlife crisis, I was about to find out, allergies or not. My quest to go over the mountain had begun.

2. Getting Ready to Reach New Heights

April - December, 2010

I was far from ready to climb Mount Kilimanjaro when I decided to attempt it in early 2010. I had a lot to do if I was going to reach the summit of Africa's highest mountain. I first needed to assemble a team to join me, hire a guide, and put together the right gear. Then I had to stay healthy and prepare myself physically and mentally for the grueling journey ahead.

Thousands of climbers have climbed Kilimanjaro since the first team reached the top in 1889. Back then, German professor Hans Meyer and Austrian mountaineer Ludwig Purtscheller, with the help of a local guide, two tribal headmen, nine porters, and a cook, broke through ice fields to reach the summit. The large glaciers that once covered the peak receded over time, so the ascent was no longer as treacherous as it once was. Climbing Kilimanjaro did not require advanced technical skills or special gear, although it was still quite challenging for first-time climbers like me unused to high-altitude trekking. The mountain has been called "Everyman's Everest" because it's considered one of the easiest of the "Seven Summits," the highest peaks on each of the world's seven continents. However, it was by no means an easy climb. A friend of mine who made it to the top said, "It's easy, man. When I did it, there was a huge snowstorm so bad that I had to help some of the porters get down. No sweat! It's a piece of cake."

"Yeah, right," I chuckled. According to my wife, Mount Kilimanjaro was more difficult than childbirth. I believed her. Many climbers failed to reach the summit. Each year climbers died or were severely injured on the mountain as a result of altitude sickness, rockslides or exposure to the elements. Just two weeks before I planned to set out for my own climb, former tennis star Martina Navratilova was evacuated from Kilimanjaro after succumbing to altitude sickness. Even one of the best tennis players of all time did not make it. It was unwise for me to underestimate the risks involved. My physical condition was a far cry from that of a sports champion, and I wasn't close to being in the shape I needed to be in to climb. I wasn't as afraid of the prospect of death as I was of getting to the summit and back safely with my health intact.

I needed good teammates to share the experience. I wished my wife could have joined me, but Jing had already climbed Kilimanjaro, and we couldn't leave our young son alone over the holidays to go on a risky venture. I planned the trip without her. I put out a call to colleagues and friends to join the team. Betty, Kay and Tom responded. We hardly knew each other when we banded together to attempt Kilimanjaro but soon got to know each other. A few other people dropped out not long before the trip. I grew concerned that we would not have a large enough group to do the climb, but as it turned out, four was just fine. Our motley crew had the same chance of making it to the summit as a larger team.

None of us was young or a seasoned mountaineer, but we seemed to have the drive and resolve to succeed. Although some were more fit than others, the mountain would affect each of us differently, and we had no way of knowing who among us, if anyone, would suffer an injury or altitude sickness on the climb.

Betty was our Kilimanjaro veteran. The Zambian tried to reach the top three years earlier but had to turn around when altitude sickness and blindness overwhelmed her just short of the summit. Betty dreamed of planting her country's flag at the top of Uhuru Peak, a vision that prompted her to try again. She said, "I want to make Zambia proud. Africans don't usually pay to go on these kinds of climbs, but that's because we're smart. Who wants to spend a lot of money to be miserable on a mountain? I'm doing this for my country."

Betty grumbled that on her earlier attempt other climbers mistook her for a worker. She said with a fiery look in her eyes, "Someone ordered me to bring him water while I was in camp. Can you imagine that? The man thought I was a porter! He was surprised when I said that I was like him."

Kay, the athletic, no-nonsense member of our team, had never summited a mountain like Kilimanjaro but ran many marathons and road races. An avid runner, she whipped herself into excellent shape before the climb by maintaining a robust training regimen. I sometimes saw her jogging by the side of the road as I drove around Lusaka, a reminder that I needed to be more disciplined. She was more than ready to tackle Kilimanjaro.

A vegetarian armed with an array of energy snacks, Kay was ready to teach me how to survive on a meatless diet and to offer me an energy boost whenever I needed one. She hailed from the same part of the United States as me, and we shared many a story of life in our former haunts. As she was single, we joked that she would find love on the trail and meet a retired Scandinavian gentleman named "Thor."

Tom, the seasoned adventurer, had been on hiking trips around the world but never climbed a mountain as mighty as Kilimanjaro. Nicknamed "Indiana Jones" by his sister-in-law after an earlier trek through the Himalayas, Tom was full of stories of life in exotic places. A jovial guy, he had a great sense of humor and always kept us laughing with moments of levity. He had in mind to tackle Kilimanjaro after years living in Africa but never had the opportunity to do so until he joined our group. While not as athletic as Kay, he was in better shape than me and showed considerable moxie when he hiked. Tom gave up a comfortable holiday in Europe with his family to join us. I was honored that he passed on sipping wine in Paris to freeze with me in thin air.

I was the young guy on the team, although my age did not give me any particular advantage. I had never climbed a mountain and was not athletically inclined. The challenge of Kilimanjaro was far greater than any physical activity I had done before. I tried to prepare by hiking, biking, swimming and running as much as I could, but at times, I was concerned that it wasn't enough. I did some activities for the first time, including my first mini-triathlon and a scuba diving experience that left me with a bout of schistosomiasis, a parasitic disease that I treated with prescription drugs. Exercising and training helped me lose weight and put on some muscle, but not as much as I would have liked.

The team trained together regularly for a couple months to get ready. Although we didn't conquer any mountains, we mastered the rolling hills and plateaus near Lusaka. I was used to living more than 1,300 meters (4,250 feet) above sea level and thought the height would help me adjust quickly to the higher altitude on Kilimanjaro. Each weekend, Betty, Kay, Tom and I gathered at a large ranch out of town and set out on long walks, crossing equestrian paths and a small creek en route to a hiking trail that weaved through the backcountry. The green forests with fields of grassland, wildflowers, and rich brown soil were a poignant backdrop for our hikes. We trekked, sometimes in line or in small groups, and chatted about nothing in particular, occasionally lapsing into silence. Sometimes we had to look for Tom when he wandered off talking on his cell phone. I preferred the quiet stillness of nature.

We had our fair share of adventures in the Zambian

countryside. One time, we set out in sunshine and ran into a torrential downpour that sent us scurrying for shelter in the trees. We returned to the ranch drenched, and the kindly owner invited us in for tea and biscuits. We sat down under a covered patio on some waterproof patio furniture that whisked away the rain and sweat and chatted for a couple hours with her and her husband, Guy Scott, who, unbeknownst to us at the time, later became Zambia's vice president. It was a memorable visit.

On another occasion, we hiked past the home of Kenneth Kaunda, Zambia's founding father and its first president. He had a modest single-story house in the countryside with a beautiful view of the valley. When I tried to take a photo of it, Betty warned me with a hiss, "Don't do that or they'll arrest you!" I heeded her advice and put away my camera.

During another hike, we marched through the bush and ran into a bright green snake lying in our path. Betty spotted the serpent first and began to hyperventilate. Then I saw it. My heart skipped a beat. Startled, I whispered anxiously to Kay and Tom, "What should we do?"

Tom nodded over his shoulder, and we slowly backed away. Paralyzed with fear, Betty did not move. We studied it for a moment. The reptile looked at us with his lidless eye, and I couldn't tell whether it looked more afraid of us than we were of it. I asked Kay and Tom quietly, "Do you think it's a green mamba?"

"I don't really know," Tom answered. "It could be an African green snake."

Green snakes and green mambas were worlds apart in terms of lethalness. The former had a nasty but harmless bite, while the latter was among the most venomous of all snakes. The one we saw could have been either. Zambia has some of the world's deadliest snakes, from cobras to the deadly black mambas.

We waited a few minutes for the reptile to pass, but it sat motionless in our path. We debated whether to make our way around it or turn back. Either way, we did not have a prayer of outrunning the serpent if it were a mamba. Finally, I said, "Let me see if I can get around him."

I made a wide berth around the snake and eased by it, careful not to make any sudden movements. After I passed, it slithered into the bush. I breathed a sigh of relief. The others followed me cautiously. I later discovered that we had encountered a harmless green snake. I shuddered to think what might have happened if it had been a mamba.

After nine months of rigorous training, I thought that I stood a good chance of reaching the top of Kilimanjaro. Although I did not do any practice climbs or transform myself into a finely tuned athlete, I shed about ten kilograms (22 pounds) and put some muscle on my legs. Nevertheless, I was not in the shape in which I wanted to be as the climb approached. Every extra pound I carried would go up and down the mountain with me like a weight belt. I trained as much as I could, but I knew that my success ultimately depended on how well my body adapted to higher altitudes.

The group met a few times to discuss our trip. We needed a good outfitter, an experienced company or guide that knew the mountain intimately and could lead a bunch of novice climbers like us safely to the summit and back. I researched operators and shortlisted a few that offered their services at a decent price. Most companies charged between US$1,500 and US$7,500 for a seven-day climbing package that included a team of guides, porters, and cooks. We opted to hire a more affordable outfitter instead of the "gold-plated deluxe package" offered by some operators. I figured that the extra cost was for state-of-the-art equipment and creature comforts that would make little difference on the mountain. I wanted to have a good trip but wasn't about to pay three times more to climb the same route. I budgeted US$3,000 for the guide, park entrance fee, airfare, lodging, meals, and the obligatory "I Climbed Kilimanjaro" T-shirt after I finished. I actually paid about US$3,500, less than most climbers because flying from Lusaka was cheaper than coming in from another continent.

We narrowed our choice of outfitters to two and finally settled on August, a small, independent operator who guided my wife and her group on their Kilimanjaro climb. A few of them recommended August, calling him "helpful" and his operation "no frills." If he helped my wife get there and back, I thought, then surely he was good enough for us. He charged a reasonable fee but offered fewer amenities than some outfitters.

We planned to ring in the New Year on the summit in memorable fashion. While billions of people would celebrate New Year's Day 2011 in the lowlands with fireworks and fanfare, I wanted to be on top of the world. August recommended that we arrive in Tanzania on Christmas Day, but leaving our families on a holiday was not an option, so we decided to depart the next morning and shorten our trip to nine days, with seven days of trekking and two in transit. We would lose an extra day adjusting to the high altitude, but being with family on Christmas was more important. We had already run the risk that we wouldn't succeed by climbing during the rainy season, rather than during one of the dry seasons in January-March and June-October. We faced the prospect of heavy snow and rain in December, but standing on the summit on New Year's, exactly one year to the day after my wife ascended, made the risk worth it.

With our outfitter in place and dates set, I turned my attention to begging, borrowing, or buying clothing and equipment. An avid shopper and Kilimanjaro veteran, Jing helped me gear up as if it were her personal mission to ensure my success. She lent me hand-me-downs from her own climb. Her jacket was too small for my big frame, but her sturdy daypack, pair of hiking poles, and gaiters that wrapped around my legs like cowboy chaps suited me fine. I planned to take so much of her clothing and gear back to the mountain that I might as well have taken her too.

Before we went shopping, Jing rattled off a long list of clothing and equipment that I needed to buy. She left me mesmerized as she spoke with authority, her advice coming at me like an avalanche. "It's all about layers. You need different layers of clothing so you can take them off or put them on when you climb. Start with thermal underwear and long johns and add water-resistant sweats and a shirt. Then wear a light jacket under your parka."

"Yes, dear," was the only response I could muster. I was glad that the best climber in our family, my wife, was helping me make sure I was prepared.

We visited various sporting goods stores in Zambia and South Africa to buy what we could. Although they sold a wide range of gear that catered to locals going camping, fishing or on safari, their selection of climbing equipment and alpine clothing was sparse.

What little they did carry was very expensive, presumably because few people living in Southern Africa were climbers. Jing and I waited to shop until we went to the United States. The others leaned on friends and relatives to line up whatever they needed.

Happy to have an excuse to go shopping, my wife sprang to action during our trip to America, taking me to several outfitters and sporting goods stores to purchase clothing and gear. Walking through store after store, my mountaineering fashion coach paced the aisles like a drill sergeant and pointed out what I needed with a sweep of her hand. I followed her around like a puppy, occasionally wandering off when something else caught my attention. Halting in the footwear section, she told me with a seriousness that grabbed my attention, "Hey, stay with me. You need to pick some hiking boots. Good boots are one of most important things you can buy. Take your time and choose the right ones. Make sure they fit you and are really comfortable on the trail."

A store clerk helped me narrow down my choices to two. The variety was mind-boggling, yet they all looked the same. I scanned the long line of boots priced well above US$150 per pair and wondered whether the premium brands and styles offered added comfort and durability that made the additional cost worthwhile. I picked up a few, smelled them, rubbed them, and looked them over. I almost licked them but stopped myself. Intimidated, I threw the boots in disgust into a pile and started to walk away. Jing pulled me back and made me focus on the task at hand. I was never a good shopper and was not as interested in hunting for my own gear as I should have been, so having a shopping guru by my side helped me get through the ordeal. Whenever I tired of wandering the aisles and started whining like a kid, she reminded me, "Hey, I'm doing this for you! You need the right gear, so work with me."

Jing set me straight. I tried on a few pairs and settled on a comfortable, mid-priced pair of Keen boots. I also chose a thick North Face jacket that would have kept me warm in outer space. I accessorized my alpine wardrobe with layer after layer of thermal underwear and shirts made from high-tech synthetic fabrics that wicked water or sweat away from the body, rain or shine. I left the store with two heavy sacks filled with enough clothing to dress a penguin colony.

Most of the snow and ice on Kilimanjaro was long gone, so I skipped buying mountaineering equipment. I passed on the ice ax, ropes, crampons, or other accessories I would have needed on more difficult ascents. A sturdy set of hiking boots and a pair of hiking poles were all that was required to make it to the summit.

With my team, outfitter, and gear squared away, I still had plenty to do. I lined up round-trip plane tickets from Lusaka to Arusha, the largest city near Mount Kilimanjaro. I booked rooms at hotels in Arusha for the inbound and outbound travel days, assuming that we were going to need a good night's sleep before the climb and a place to rest and recuperate after we finished. I also lined up a visa to enter Tanzania. With those preparations done, I was almost set for my trip. All I needed to do was pack and stay healthy.

My optimism that I had a fair chance of reaching the summit evaporated when my health deteriorated. In early November 2011, less than two months before the climb, I came down with a terrible flu that lingered for weeks. The fever and sweaty chills passed after several days in bed, but my deep cough, tight chest and constricted breathing persisted. I stopped exercising and made frequent visits to see the nurse. My condition worsened a few weeks later when the rainy season started, the heavy downpours and flash flooding kicking up dust, mold, mildew, pollen and other particles that settled in my lungs and left me with a choking cough. By early

December, just two weeks before the climb, I was so sick that I began to wonder whether I should cancel it. I begged the nurse to give me anything that would bring me back to health in a hurry. The antibiotics and inhalers had a limited effect on my respiratory system; the reading on the small device I used to measure my lung capacity was well below normal. If I couldn't breathe properly at lower altitudes, I lamented, I would probably struggle in thin air. My December 26 departure date loomed like an imminent disaster.

I needed to revive my health if I was going to have any hope of challenging Mount Kilimanjaro. Africa's highest peak promised any number of maladies, aches, pains, and infirmities to make my experience miserable. Most climbers were susceptible to at least one ailment, and many considered it a badge of honor to come down with something on the trail. I expected blisters or lost toenails, sunburns, strained or sore muscles, but I was more concerned that my respiratory issue would leave me vulnerable to more serious conditions such as acute mountain sickness (AMS) and its sometimes lethal cousins, high altitude cerebral edema (HACE) and high altitude pulmonary edema (HAPE). I took along a week's worth of Diamox, a drug that helped prevent altitude sickness, to fend off illness but shied away from using it because of its nasty side effects, including numbness and tingling in the fingers and toes, loss of appetite, bad taste in the mouth, and blurred vision.

My health problems loomed large as the climb approached. Medicine and inhalers helped but did not bring me back to full health. I was still coughing and had a tight chest a couple days before the trip. A year's worth of effort to climb on the rooftop of Africa came down to whether I could breathe.

3. 'Twas the Night before the Climb

December 25, 2010

My family and I enjoyed a quiet Christmas in Lusaka with my in-laws. Our neighbors invited us over to celebrate with friends and colleagues, a nice gesture considering how far away we were from family in the United States. Zambia's warm climate did not lend itself to the season. There was no snow, and few Zambians had the means to put up displays of holiday cheer such as Christmas trees, decorations, or presents. It was a gift that I could enjoy the holiday with my loved ones on the eve of my departure.

I mingled and chatted at the party, munching on rich foods that I knew I would miss on the mountain. I did my best to hide the fact that I still did not feel well. Friends peppered me with questions about my trip and asked what I had done to prepare, and I smiled and answered them as upbeat as I could. Their well wishes made me feel better. A colleague lent me his knit stocking cap when I told him that I couldn't find mine stored away in a box somewhere in my house. We didn't need winter clothing in snow-free Zambia.

The nurse I visited so many times joined the party. We sat together and talked for a while. Although we avoided specifics, our conversation inevitably crept back to Kilimanjaro and whether I was well enough to climb.

"How are you feeling?" she asked. I forced a smile and let out a nervous chuckle that ended with a small cough. "I'm fine. I think I'll be okay."

I did my best to conceal my illness, but her sharp eyes probed my façade, searching for the real answer. She looked concerned. I wondered whether I was in denial and headed for a disaster. I looked down and nibbled on some *injera*, an Ethiopian sponge bread.

"Are you positive?"

I recalled our last meeting in her office. I said again, "Yes, I'm sure."

"Okay, then," she said with finality. She switched the subject to healthy eating as we feasted on a smorgasbord of Christmas delights.

I trudged home later while the rest of the family stayed behind. I needed some time alone to think and pack. The looming trip dampened my normally festive holiday mood. Climbing a mountain seemed like a good idea until I actually had to do it. I remembered looking in Kilimanjaro's direction on New Year's Day the year before, wondering whether my wife reached the summit. When she called me the next day to tell me that she made it, I was so impressed with her feat that she inspired me to give it a try. One year later, my heart was heavy. I wanted to climb in her footsteps and experience the thrill as she had, but I wondered when the time came whether I would have the courage and resolve to go through with it.

I weighed my travel options. I still had time to cancel, even though I would have had to absorb some of the cost; it would be a small price to pay compared to suffering a catastrophe on the Kilimanjaro. I could cut my trip short if I ran into trouble and go on safari in one of the nearby game reserves. That wasn't an option if I pushed myself too hard and had to be evacuated from the mountain. The prospect of lying in a hospital bed being treated for altitude sickness or another ailment did not sit well with me. If I went ahead with the climb, I had to listen to my body and turn back before it was too late.

I wondered what Hemingway's protagonist in *The Snows of Kilimanjaro*, Harry, would have done in my situation. Lying on a cot in the shadow of the mountain, dying from an infected leg wound, surrounded by blood-thirsty hyenas and birds ready to devour his body, he faced a similar dilemma of whether to keep fighting or give up and let go. In the end, Harry surrendered and perished. I refused to do that. I would rise to the challenge and overcome it.

I couldn't do it alone. I prayed for health and a safe trip. I was told that I didn't need a god to climb Kilimanjaro and that many climbers reached the summit without leaning on a higher power. That didn't matter to me. I found it personally comforting to know that God would be with me on this journey. He was always there for me, even during the difficult times that fueled my midlife crisis. I learned to rely on someone greater than me when the burden was too heavy to bear.

In the evening after my family returned home, Jing helped me organize and pack my gear. We debated whether to use a duffel bag, backpack, or suitcase, how many, and what mix. I decided to use a large duffel bag, mid-size travel bag, and a daypack. If I carried my own luggage, I would have used one large backpack, but August's porters were going to haul the large items up the mountain for me while I carried the daypack. Jing placed the luggage on the floor and sorted through piles of clothing and equipment, saying over and over, "You're going to need this. And that. And this too."

I marveled as I watched her work. I could not have asked for a better Christmas present from my wife than her help getting me ready for my climb. How I wished I could have taken her with me! I tried to put the gear into whichever tote I could find room but did a poor job of it. When I stuffed one half full of food, she said, "Hon, you don't really need all that. You won't eat it all. Everything you don't eat will come back with you. Take some out and make your bag lighter."

Jing made sure that I packed the right items in optimal quantities. I did not object; after all, her experience on Kilimanjaro made her imminently qualified to weigh in on what I should bring. She did a masterful job helping me pack what I needed without overdoing it. I appreciated her expertise.

My wife suddenly stopped and looked at me. "Are you sure you're okay?"

"Yes. Why do you ask?"

"You look a little pale. Are you sure you're okay to climb?" she asked me one last time. She must have seen in my face the shade of illness I tried to hide. No matter what I said, she knew I wasn't feeling well.

Now was the time to decide if I was going to do the climb. I pondered her question for a moment. I still had not fully recovered, but I was reluctant to pull out of a trip I had invested so much effort into organizing and abandon my climbing partners. Everything was set in motion. I needed to do it, I decided. For me.

"Hon, I'm okay. Don't worry. I'm ready to do this."

I was going to Tanzania. My fate was sealed.

4. Kilimanjaro Beckons

December 26, 2010

The day after Christmas, Jing, my son, and I drove to Lusaka International Airport to rendezvous with my travel companions. Kay and Tom arrived solo, while Betty's family and friends came with her to say goodbye with a big Zambian-style send-off. I gave my wife and son hugs and kisses at the gate. They said they would pray for me and wished me well. As I walked away, my wife waved and shouted, "Let's talk after you reach the summit!"

"Okay!" I told her above the fray as I entered the gate with my bags in tow. This must have been like what soldiers went through every time they said goodbye to their families before being deployed. Mount Kilimanjaro was by no means a battlefield, although it was going to be a struggle. It certainly felt like I was getting ready to do battle with the mountain.

I passed through check-in and headed to the small airport café to wait for my flight. Kay and Tom were seated at a table, eating and drinking coffee. I joined them and ordered an African-style English breakfast of eggs, sausage, baked beans, stewed tomatoes, and white bread. I ate the heavy meal anticipating that I would consume a week's worth of gruel and mush. Tom had the same. I told him, "You know, this breakfast might not sit well with us."

"Yeah, but it sure tastes good!" He laughed. I chortled. Tom was always good for some early morning humor. He stroked his scholarly beard like a professor and flashed a wild twinkle in his eye.

Kay dined on a light vegetarian meal and smiled at us. She sipped her coffee and cut some melon with a table knife. Setting it next to her toast, she lifted the melon with her fork and said with a hint of sarcasm, winking at us, "Fruit is much easier on the stomach."

She was right, of course. Her subtle humor always seemed to bear a kernel of truth. Betty arrived as the loudspeaker announced that our flight was boarding. We gobbled up the rest of our food, emptied our cups, and headed to the gate.

The sights and sounds of Africa filled the airport lounge. Large, multi-generational families mingled with Catholic nuns. Women in short shorts, tight tank tops, flashy manicures, and neon stilettoes stood next to Muslim women in veiled *niqab* and men in *thowb* robes, *kufi* hats, and *keffiyeh* headdresses. Chinese men — all men, as far as I could tell — wearing dark slacks, leather belts, and light cotton knit shirts huddled together in tight circles, smoking their last cigarettes before departure. *Muzungu,* or westerners, and locals of African and South Asian descent sat in the worn plastic seats that lined the concrete walls of the 1960s-era terminal. Our team fit right in with the unkempt *muzungu* backpackers wearing faded T-shirts, shorts and sandals, who stood in clusters around the room with their carry-on bags slung over their shoulders. The smell of body odor permeated the air. I coughed, the stale air irritating my lungs. I reached for my inhaler.

I didn't ogle the crowd long before we heard the call to board our flight. We rushed through the door and stampeded toward the jet plane that sat on the tarmac not far from the building. I passed some passengers who were strolling leisurely toward it; a few impatient souls cut in front of me. Even on an airplane with assigned seating, we still competed for space. It seemed ingrained in the local psyche to jockey for position and take what you could get whenever the opportunity presented itself.

We boarded the plane bound for Dar Es Salaam, Tanzania. I

read and slept most of the way, munching on a small sandwich and crisps provided by the airline, an incidental meal considering the steep price I paid for a ticket. The plane circled Dar on the descent, giving us a spectacular aerial view of the city.

The aircraft landed with a thud at Julius Nyerere International Airport and dumped us on the international side. Our group followed a throng of passengers through immigration and customs and collected our luggage, then puzzled over where to find the connecting flight to Arusha. We wandered around the terminal for a few minutes until we located the gate on the domestic side of the airport. Exiting the building, we were met by a gaggle of taxi drivers and hawkers waiting to accost us in rudimentary English with offers of glorious bargains. "You want ride to city? Where you going? I take you!"

"No thanks, no thanks," I chanted as if in prayer, bowing my head to avoid their eyes and pressing on. I pushed through the crowd to the security checkpoint that blocked the domestic entrance. Playing it safe, I tucked my wallet and wristwatch into my daypack before sending it through the scanner. I made it through the x-ray machine without setting it off but piqued the interest of the security officer, who grinned and said, "I like your hat."

He pointed at the baseball cap on my head. I was not sure whether he meant it as a pleasantry or had designs on it. Suspecting the latter, I smiled and thanked him in Swahili, "Asante sana."

He waited as if expecting me to give him my hat, so I feigned ignorance. Pointing at his beret, I winked and said, "I like yours too."

He declined to exchange hats and waved me on. I joined the others at check-in. The ticketing agent told us that an earlier flight had space available if we wanted to fly to Arusha ahead of schedule, and we decided to take her up on the offer. I tried to contact August to let him know we would arrive early but could not reach him.

The one-and-a-half hour flight to Arusha offered an amazing bird's eye view of the Kilimanjaro region with its rolling hills and rugged terrain. Decaying extinct volcanic peaks worn with age rose up amid brown fields and green forests that passed below my double-paned window flaked with frost. In less than 24 hours I would be down there, somewhere, hiking. I started coughing lightly from the stale cabin air, or perhaps, from the reminder that I would soon be going on a long trek.

"Hey, I can see it!" Tom said from across the aisle. "I see Kili."

I tried to catch a glimpse of Mount Kilimanjaro, also nicknamed "Kili," through the window on his side of the plane but couldn't see it. A peak as massive as Kilimanjaro should have been easy to see, even with other *grande dames* such as Mount Kenya and Mount Meru dotting the horizon. I didn't mind. The mountain and I would get acquainted soon enough.

The jet stream buffeted our aircraft with turbulent headwinds that left my stomach queasy, but the descent was smooth. We landed at Kilimanjaro International Airport, an airstrip on a plain to the south of its namesake. Crossing the tarmac, we passed through the quaint terminal and were curbside in minutes. August's team had not yet arrived, and he didn't answer when I tried to call him to let him know we were ready for pick up. We debated whether to save our money and wait for him or hire a shuttle van to take us to the hotel. Betty arranged transportation for US$20 per person; three extra hours of rest at the hotel were worth the cost. We would meet our guide at the lodge.

Betty, Kay, Tom and I did not talk much as the van sped through the countryside toward Arusha. The landscape reminded me of Zambia. The flat, semiarid steppes near the airport gave way to subtropical forest as we drove near the mountain. Capped by three volcanic cones, Kibo, Mawenzi, and Shira, Kilimanjaro was so massive that its sheer size influenced climate patterns, forcing the clouds to dump precipitation on its flanks and pass over the plain with nary a drop. Located in a subtropical bowl between Mount Kilimanjaro and its sister, Mount Meru, the city of Arusha sat in the middle of an overgrown rain forest on the wet side of the mountain.

As the countryside gave way to city, the shuttle passed row after row of single-story strip malls with bright façades and colorful names like the "Obama Bar." The view from my window offered an entertaining look at the unique sights, sounds and colors of Africa. Arusha spread out organically, as if osmosis had taken it wherever there were spots on which to build. Streets followed lines of shade trees with no apparent rhyme or reason. Sleek high-rise hotels stood next to low-slung, ramshackle cement buildings filled with small family businesses whose only advertisements were hand-painted signs with clever names. In the city center lay a few nondescript government buildings dominated by the International Criminal Tribunal of Rwanda, a United Nations court set up to prosecute criminals involved in the 1994 Rwanda genocide.

In the early afternoon, the bus taxi dropped us off at our lodge, the *Arusha Tourist Inn*, after taking an inadvertent detour to its sister property, the *Arusha Tourist Centre Inn*. The no-frills, US$45-per-night lodge filled with backpackers and climbers half my age was adequate for the outbound portion of our trip. I needed to get used to roughing it because accommodations on the mountain were going to be much less comfortable.

I felt fatigued after traveling all day. After checking in, the group agreed to meet again for dinner. I trudged to my room and hauled my luggage up two flights of stairs, letting the bags bounce and scrape on the floor. The sound echoed through the hall like a dull drum. Pushing the door open with my foot, I pulled my cargo into the tidy, sparsely furnished room, which was none too well lit. I tossed my belongings in a corner and crashed on the small bed. My chest felt heavy when I lay down, so I rummaged through my bags for my inhaler. I hadn't been coughing but needed to stay on top of it before it got the best of me. Settled in, I rested my eyes.

I woke up an hour later and called August. He answered and told me that he was waiting for us at the airport. I apologized that he made a needless trip and asked him if he would meet us at the lodge. He agreed to join us at suppertime. I knew after numerous back and forths with August that he had taken our impromptu change of plans in stride. His guiding philosophy seemed to be what I called "hakuna matata," a Swahili term meaning "no worries" that was popularized by Disney's film "The Lion King." I thought him a "don't worry, be happy" kind of person who apparently accepted whatever life threw at him without letting it upset his equilibrium. Our guide seemed to handle problems with such a cool head that he left the impression he was in control of any situation. I soon realized that his tendency to be disorganized and reactive sometimes made his life more difficult.

In the evening, Betty, Kay, Tom and I met for dinner at the inn's faux Bavarian restaurant. The kitschy Alpine interior looked like an overzealous attempt to appeal to Europeans or to those who were nostalgic for the German flavor still lingering in Tanzania, a former colony. The dim lights in the dining room that tried to mimic the ambiance of a Bavarian beer hall softened the room's dated appearance. German beer advertisements lined the solitary wall not dominated by street windows, the front desk, or the kitchen. We sat down at a wooden table covered with a red-and-white checkered tablecloth. The one-page menu offered a variety of continental European dishes. I ordered Hungarian *goulash* and *spaetzle*, bite-size dumplings that made a delicious alternative to pasta or rice. I knew that I shouldn't indulge in such a heavy meal the night before the climb but relished the chance to eat one of my favorite dishes. I had plenty of chances to do without on Kilimanjaro. Downing a draught of beer, I threw out a question to my companions. "So, are you all ready to do this?"

"Definitely. I'm more than ready," Kay said.

"Sure I am. I think it's going to be a good trip," Tom chimed in.

"Yes, I'm all set to go," Betty added.

"Well, then, how about a toast?" I offered. We raised our glasses and wished ourselves a successful climb. Our mugs clinked with a sweet sound that signaled the start of our adventure. The cordial vibes coming from the group gave me hope that we would succeed. We bonded over the past few months as we trained together, and our camaraderie would help us achieve our main objective — to stand together on the rooftop of Africa. I stood a better chance of reaching the summit with a team to support me when the going got tough than doing it alone.

August walked in as we ate. A silent, gentle presence, he said hello with a warm smile.

"August!" I exclaimed. I stood up and shook his hand. "So nice to see you! Come have a seat with us."

The group gave him a hearty welcome. This was the first time the others had seen or talked to him. I had been in touch with our guide for months making plans, and I'd seen photos of him guiding my wife's team last year, but this was our first face-to-face meeting. Sitting down, August said, "Welcome, friends. Let me show you the route we will take. Please ask me any questions you may have."

He spread out a worn-out map of Kilimanjaro on the table. Then he traced our path with his finger. The invisible line started on the north side of the mountain, went to the summit, then headed south and ended almost 90 kilometers (55 miles) away from the starting point. He said, "We will hike up the Rongai and then down the Marangu. The trip will be seven days starting tomorrow and end on January 2."

"Is that the best route to take?" Tom asked. "What about the other ones?"

I decided to climb via the Rongai Route, the same one my wife's group took, because I knew they had reached the summit — and for sentimental reasons. I wanted to follow in Jing's footsteps. I lobbied hard for the Rongai, and the others went along.

August explained that each trail was different and had its own advantages and disadvantages. There was no one best way to trek Mount Kilimanjaro. Most climbers chose to follow the Marangu Route, also known as the "Coca-Cola" Route, because it was a longer and more gradual way to reach Kibo Huts, a base camp below the summit. Some considered the Marangu the easiest, as it offered a smoother trek and gave climbers more time to acclimatize to the high altitude. Our guide pointed out that the Machame Route, or "Whiskey Route," and the Umbwe, or "Vodka Route," were hard and fast ascents with little time to acclimatize and thus riskier because they lowered climbers' odds of reaching the summit. The way was more direct and better for those who adjusted quicker to higher altitudes. August said that the Shira-Lemosho, a longer, lesser-used track, was akin to a walking safari with frequent animal sightings. Guides there were required to carry firearms in the event trekkers stumbled upon a predator. Running into a wild animal on the adventure of my life was not the kind of heart-pounding excitement I needed.

The Rongai trailhead, where we would begin our climb, was more than three hours from Arusha on the north side of Kilimanjaro, close to the Kenyan border. The other trails started much closer to the city. August told us that the path was moderately steep, relatively sheltered from the elements in a drier part of the mountain, less crowded, and scenic with Alpine vistas. I dubbed the Rongai the "Kilimanjaro Beer" Route because it lay somewhere between a Coca-Cola and a whiskey shot in terms of potency.

August pointed out that we could change our route at the last minute, so we pored over the map and debated which trail to use. We were too late to take the Shira-Lemosho or the Northern Circuit Route that circled the mountain since they took two extra days. He dissuaded us from taking the Umbwe because it required a higher level of endurance and technical skill to scale the mountain face. The Marangu and Machame were viable alternatives, but in the end we stayed with the plan to take the Rongai uphill and the Marangu downhill.

We pelted August with questions about the climb and what to expect. Kay asked, "What about sleeping arrangements?"

"You can use a double tent or pay more for a single," he answered. Betty and Kay agreed to share a double while Tom and I opted to sleep in our own tents.

"What about the weather conditions on the mountain?" Betty asked.

"The weather is good right now, and the conditions are favorable for our climb," the guide said in his no-nonsense manner. He added, "However, the forecast calls for rain and possibly snow for the next few days."

Observing the mugs of half-drunk beers on the table, August cautioned, "It's not a good idea to drink alcohol before a climb because it can heighten the effects of altitude sickness."

Oops. I had already made a mistake. I took his warning in stride and finished off my last beer, not wanting to let a good brew go to waste.

After half an hour of relentless interrogation, August answered all of our questions. I invited him to join us for dinner, but he said that he needed to go home to say goodbye to his family. He asked us to be ready to leave early the next morning and bade us good night. He left me with the impression we were in good hands with him, although time would tell whether I was right.

As we wrapped up dinner, two Danish women sat down and introduced themselves as Birgit and Laura. They told us that they had returned from the mountain earlier in the day. Beaming, they announced that they had reached the summit via the Machame Route. We congratulated them with a toast. I asked, "So how did it go?"

"Great! It wasn't as bad as I thought," said Birgit. "It was actually quite easy."

"Wow, easy? Tell us what happened," I said, surprised. I wondered whether we should have chosen the Machame until they rattled off horror stories about freezing weather, snow in their tents at base camp, and feeling so isolated that it sounded as if they had been sent to solitary confinement. I asked if they used music or other entertainment to fend off the loneliness, and Birgit answered, "Oh, no, I just listened to the sounds of the mountain. Kili kept me company."

Laura added that their climb ended on a bad note when they were nearly robbed in Arusha's main square, not long after another tourist was injured in an attack by would-be thieves. I made a mental note not to wander around town.

I retired to my room early in the evening. The light from the solitary desk lamp was so faint that I could barely distinguish anything in the cramped quarters. I propped open the bathroom door and turned on the light to brighten the room up a bit, but it was still too dim. I found the headlamp, with its strong beam capable of illuminating a trail in the dark of night, and wrapped it around my forehead like a miner. The small beam lit up a small circle wherever I moved my head; not a perfect solution but good enough.

I opened my luggage and scattered my belongings in piles to reorganize them in a way that would make it easy for me to locate items when I needed them in a tent or on the trail. I set aside clothing for the next day and for our return to Arusha and put the rest in protective, re-sealable plastic sacks that looked like oversized freezer bags. The trekking gear went into my travel bag, the clothing and food in the duffle bag, and a few items I would need for the day, including two one-liter bottles filled with water, some snacks, toilet paper, and my iPod music player, in the daypack. I decided to hike the first day in tennis shoes because the forecast called for good weather, and I preferred to wait to put on my hiking boots until I needed them.

The sound outside my room's paper-thin walls grew noisier as the evening turned to night. The walls reverberated with the din of besotted drinkers inebriated in the Bavarian restaurant and of lost souls who wandered the halls. The passersby who walked through the street below were a loud bunch, especially the drunken man who yelled unintelligibly in the alleyway behind the hotel at four a.m. I was curious what all the hubbub was about but thought it better to remain ensconced in my room and try to get a good night's sleep.

After I squared away my packing, I cleaned up and settled into bed, pulling the mosquito net around me and checking the interior for wayward pests. The net covered the bed like a tent, hanging from the ceiling so low that I could not sit upright without becoming tangled in it. Lying in bed, I switched on my headlamp, propped my head up with one hand, and studied a trio of laminated signs that I made to commemorate the climb. If all went well and I made it the summit, I would display them in front of the iconic wooden Kilimanjaro sign. One placard read, "Hello Family & Friends, I Did It." The second said, "I Made It" and the third "Hello Naysayers' Club, I Did It," a nod to those who helped trigger my mid-life crisis. Taking photos with these signs on the rooftop of Africa was a great motivator.

I thought about my family and wondered how they were doing. I sent my wife a text message on my cell phone to let her know that I had made it safely to Arusha. Then I turned on my Kindle e-reader and recorded details of my trip in my journal. The device had a handy notepad program that let me input my thoughts electronically. As I started to write about my first day of travel, my mind wandered, contemplating all that transpired to this point. Even though I already devoted months preparing for the climb and fighting illness, my journey had only begun.

I thought about the Foreign Service and whether I should resign. The "Naysayers' Club," skeptics who were critical of me because I focused on doing a good job rather than playing sycophant, would continue to dog me if I stayed in the diplomatic corps. I needed to rise above their low opinions and leave their intimidation behind. I had to put my underrated skills to better uses, away from a culture I considered overly conformist and narcissistic. Unlike Harry, I would not wallow in misery or chafe at a frustrating reality, I decided alone in the dark. I preferred to walk away, no matter what the cost, and search for a more fulfilling life.

I tapped away on the Kindle, its backlight illuminating my words. I pondered my health. Apart from a few respiratory flare-ups, I felt better in Tanzania than I did in Zambia, as if I magically left my allergies back home. My breathing seemed to improve as soon as I landed in Arusha. I felt better than I had in months, even though my health was still fragile and I had not trained much for the past few weeks. I was cautiously optimistic that it would continue.

I ended the night with a prayer that I would overcome any obstacles in my path to reach the summit. Only God knew whether I would succeed. I prayed that I would be healthy and safe.

Whether I made it to the top and back safely also depended on me. I needed to play my part to ensure that I made it home without serious injury, or worse. I had to be careful and turn back if it became obvious that I would not make it. If fate intervened and kept me from reaching my goal, I was going to accept it. As one of the world's great mountaineers, Ed Viesturs, said so eloquently, "Getting to the top is optional. Getting down is mandatory."

I turned off the e-reader and fell into a dreamless sleep.

5. Coming Around the Mountain

December 27, 2010

I woke up early in the morning feeling refreshed and ready to hit the trail. The shower doused me in cold water, and I scrambled away from its frigid jets. The chill dampened my enthusiasm and reminded me that the journey ahead was not going to be easy. I stuck my arm into the freezing water, shut off the cold valve, and turned the hot water on full bore, which reduced the flow to a trickle. Droplets of warm liquid dripped from the showerhead. "Great," I grumbled. I wanted one last hot soaking before hitting the mountain, before a week's worth of sponge baths or no baths at all, but it didn't happen. I turned off the shower and sponge bathed instead, shivering as the cool air swirled around me.

"That's what I get for staying at a cheap inn," I groused. I had to get used to doing without the comforts and conveniences I took for granted, like warm showers, because I was going to miss them on Kilimanjaro.

I dressed and went to the Bavarian restaurant for breakfast. Although it was closed, the inn accommodated our early departure with a light spread of fruit, boiled eggs, juice and coffee. Kay joined me a few minutes later for a cup of coffee and a couple of pigmy bananas the size of a finger that she thought were "adorable and sweet." I wanted bacon.

The power went off, plunging the restaurant in darkness until an early-rising waiter lit some candles. Kay and I enjoyed breakfast by candlelight, the glow flickering on our faces, until the lights came on fifteen minutes later. They soon cut out again. Referring to the rolling brownouts we sometimes had in Lusaka, Kay remarked,

"I guess they have outages here too."

I nodded quietly. Talking took too much effort this early. Drowsiness crept in, weighing on my eyes, and the darkness tempted me to take a nap.

Tom and Betty joined us before departure. Betty complained that she had forgotten her hair dryer at home and that the inn did not have one she could borrow. She doted on her locks of hair meticulously woven into tight cornrows that fell to her shoulders and ended in braids. My slow mind could not comprehend why she made such a fuss about hair care when she was not going to use a blow dryer on the climb. A small comb to slick back my coiffure was enough for me.

I went back to my room a few minutes later, washed up, collected my luggage, and dragged it down to the front entrance where August waited with a van to take us to the mountain. I gave the duffel and travel bags to the porters but held on to my daypack. I saw the group's baggage piled in the rear of the vehicle and noticed that I brought more gear than the others. I hoped I hadn't brought too much; I thought I had packed no more than necessary.

I settled my lodging bill and hopped in the van. We departed shortly after six a.m. and made a quick detour to the Mount Meru Hotel, a newly renovated five-star palace that had recently reopened, to reserve rooms for our return trip. After a gritty climb like Kilimanjaro, I thought we would need a place to recover in style. I left a change of clothing and other items I wouldn't need until I returned with the hotel for safekeeping. I thought it better to lighten my load than take it with me.

Leaving Arusha, we drove to Moshi, a smaller city near Kilimanjaro National Park. The van stopped several times on the way so August could pick up teammates and supplies. Three porters crowded into the vehicle with us. They smiled but kept to themselves, talking to each other in Swahili. Because we didn't speak each other's language, our conversation amounted to little more than "jambo," the Swahili word for "hello," and welcoming smiles. No one in August's crew spoke English except him. I was uncomfortable knowing that August was our communication lifeline but had no alternative. He admitted that he had had difficulty finding help who spoke English. Those who knew the language usually found better jobs than being porters and cooks.

Betty, Kay, Tom and I were cloistered in the back of the van as it sped along the highway. I watched the Tanzanian landscape pass by in a blur as the vehicle drove much too fast, except when it slowed down for stop signs or speed bumps. A colorful stream of people on bicycle or foot wandered briskly along the road as if they were heading to work or school. Many turned their heads to look at us curiously when we drove past. I was certain that they had seen their fair share of foreigners packed in shuttles and busses heading to the mountain and found it entertaining, even amusing. Perhaps they wondered why climbers would spend so much time, money and effort on such a miserable endeavor.

The heat of the morning sun burned off the last of the clouds and seeped into the van's interior, warming our vinyl seats and offsetting the cool air that blew lightly from the front cab. The drive became monotonous as the scene blended together into what looked like long buildings with rust-stained corrugated aluminum roofs encircled by palms and flowering trees. I started to sweat and took off my light jacket. The ride left my stomach churning, but there was nothing I could do to soothe it. The once-pleasant trip turned into an exercise in patience.

The van stopped in Moshi to pick up some supplies and equipment. I asked August why he needed to make pickups en route rather than planning ahead, and he replied that the stores were closed on Christmas. The holiday seemed like a distant memory as I sat in the hot vehicle feeling woozy, wishing the drive were over.

We left Moshi after August and his team wrapped up their errands and headed toward the park. I saw Mount Kilimanjaro for the first time outside my window. The mountain followed the van to the park entrance, growing larger and more imposing as we drove down the road. The bulbous giant was so massive that all I could see from east to west was a huge slope covered with deep green foliage. I craned my neck to see Kibo or Mawenzi, two of its highest peaks, but they hid behind its colossal flank. Although the gently rolling ridge gave me some comfort that the climb would not be too difficult, Kilimanjaro was so enormous that I found it intimidating. It was as if an entire mountain range had been compressed into a single monster — and I had to slay it.

We stopped in the late morning at Marangu Gate, the park's main entrance, to pay our fees. I trundled out of the van, glad to breathe in fresh air after the long ride. A light breeze helped calm my uneasy stomach. We went with August to the main office, where I was surprised to learn that park management charged those who lived outside Tanzania a steep US$742 fee per person while Tanzanian residents paid just US$2.00 per day. The non-resident price included rescue service in the event of evacuation from the mountain. The fees paid for park upkeep, although climbers willing to pay whatever it cost to climb Kilimanjaro likely drove demand and inflated the price. The Tanzanians could charge whatever they wanted, and it would have made little difference in the number of mountaineers willing to pay anything to reach the summit. It was unfortunate that I lived across the border in Zambia when I could have saved hundreds of dollars if I resided in Tanzania.

We found out at the cashier that they would only accept a Visa credit card for payment. Not cash. Not check. MasterCard and other forms of credit not accepted. Visa. I recalled the company's famous tagline, *Visa, it's where you want to be*, and was grateful that I brought mine. On the mountain, that's where I wanted to be. What a great advertisement for the company to be the exclusive card of Mount Kilimanjaro. Nobody warned us ahead of time of the park's policy, and no one else in our group had the right means of payment, so I pulled out my Visa and paid almost US$3,000 for four entrance fees. If I didn't have it, we would have had to scramble to find another way to pay. I wondered how many climbers had been turned away because they didn't have the right card or tried to bribe their way onto the mountain.

Betty, Kay, and Tom reimbursed me in cash. I stashed the dollars in a small pouch slung around my neck that held my passport and wallet. I hesitated to carry so much money with me on the climb but had no other choice. The currency would come in handy when I needed to pay August and his team, or to buy snacks and drinks at the camps on the Marangu Route, but I wasn't going to spend it all on this trip. I was leery of carrying thousands of dollars all week in the wilderness and kept it close at all times.

We waited at Marangu Gate while August processed our paperwork. The clear sky and warm sun made the day pleasant, a great opportunity for a picnic if we hadn't been in a hurry to make it to the Rongai trailhead by early afternoon. Other climbers and guides on their way up or down the mountain milled around the complex. I used a flushing toilet one last time; clean latrines and bushes were the best I could hope for on the trail. I walked into the rustic-looking gift shop cluttered with items that had long collected dust and found an "I Climbed Kilimanjaro" T-shirt to buy if I reached the summit. Purchasing some snacks, I waited with the others until August finished and we hit the road. I was more than ready to get to the trailhead.

The drive through the lowlands of Kilimanjaro turned into a three-hour ordeal. The paved road gave way to gravel and dirt as it wound around the eastern side of the mountain. The van's worn shock absorbers subjected our bums to almost every bump and pothole we passed, each one we hit tossing the rear end of the vehicle into the air. The tires ploughed through the dry, soft earth where machines grated the highway to improve traction. If it had been raining, August's van might have gotten stuck in the mud like it did the year before when my wife's group traveled the same road. I wondered why the builders neglected to put down a bed of gravel to improve traction. The bumpy ride jarred that thought out of my head.

The sun overwhelmed the air conditioner and flooded the interior with warmth, leaving me uncomfortably hot. The pungent odor of sooty fumes belching from the smoking exhaust that would never have passed a vehicle inspection test seeped into the van. Hot and bothered, I held on to a handle dangling from the cab wall and tried to stifle a cough triggered by the vapor in my lungs. I struggled to suppress it, but it came out in a fit. I fought back and wrestled it under control.

I tried to take my mind off the ride by watching the landscape unfold around us. The edge of the Serengeti, a vast plain that stretched from Tanzania into Kenya, spread out below us beyond Kilimanjaro's lowlands. Forests blanketed the mountain on both sides of the road in a lush green made verdant by ample rainfall. I was glad that the land, for now, was dry and that moisture would not hamper our journey. Not yet, at least.

Betty, Kay, Tom and I chatted on the way about the climb that loomed ever closer. I pulled a map of the area from my daypack and spread it out between us. We studied it like soldiers on a battlefield, trying to assess our ground strategy. We tried to ascertain where, how far, and how high we needed to trek each day and where we would stop, estimating that we had to hike 90 kilometers (55 miles) from the Rongai trailhead back to the Marangu Gate and climb more than 3,400 meters (11,000 feet) before it was over. We laughed that if we didn't make it to the summit, then we would go on safari. Tom joked, "We might as well make lemonade if this turns into lemons."

At midday the van pulled into the village of Loitokitok, the start of the Rongai Route. I let out a cheer and hopped out of the vehicle with my daypack, careful not to spill the two full water bottles weighing it down. Betty, Kay, Tom and I headed to a picnic area to eat a quick lunch. I nibbled on a light meal of breads, fruits, and vegetables. I should have been hungry but did not have much of an appetite knowing that I was about to take my first steps on one of the longest and most difficult journeys of my life. The thought filled me with excitement and apprehension.

August rallied his 12-member team near the van. Porters tossed our bags into a pile by the side of the road while three cooks handled the propane tanks, portable stove, and large containers with food and cooking supplies. Two deputy guides chatted with August, presumably about the climb. August's team was going to support Betty, Kay, Tom, and me: four assistants for every climber. Each of us would have one guide, two porters, and a cook. It seemed excessive, but I knew that there was no way I could have focused on climbing Kilimanjaro and done their jobs too. I needed their support. I appreciated that they would haul our bags, set up our tents, prepare and serve us food, and make sure we survived the trip. Experienced mountaineers were relatively self-sufficient, but I was far from one. I just was an average person who needed all the help I could get on "Everyman's Everest." I needed to focus my attention on trekking, rather than cooking and setting up my tent. It's been said that veteran climbers who tackled mountains like Everest and K-2 sometimes ascended solo or with minimal assistance. Watching August's crew work made me appreciate their efforts all the more.

August joined us at the end of our break. When he asked us if we were ready to go, I answered, "No, not yet! We need a group photo." We gathered next to the picnic area for a shot. We were set. The time to climb had come.

6. Right Up the Rongai

December 27, 2010

We set out on the four-hour, 13-kilometer (eight mile) trek from the Rongai trailhead to Camp One, also known as Camp First Cave or Simba Camp, at about 2,700 meters (8,900 feet). The vertical rise on our first day of climbing was almost 1,800 meters (6,000 feet). Hiking conditions could not have been better. A hint of breeze swirled around me. The sky was sunny, warming the forest, but not unbearably so, with rays of sunlight that crossed our path. My wife warned me to expect wet weather, and I carried a rain poncho in my daypack, but I didn't need it while the clouds stayed to the north above the Serengeti.

The trail was dry, flat, and in great shape for a brisk hike. Stands of pine trees lined the route with such uniformity that I was certain they had been cultivated by human hands. The sight of coniferous trees made me forget for a moment that I was in Africa, where palms and savannah woods were more common, and reminded me of the wilderness trails in the United States that I used to explore. My allergies and cough seemed to vanish, and I breathed in fresh air deeper than I had in months. One day in Tanzania did wonders for my lungs. I was thrilled to feel healthy and ready to challenge the mountain.

The porters and cooks marched ahead in a long line with our bags and supplies, as August and another guide stayed behind to hike with us. I stepped aside to let the workers pass. An eclectic bunch, they dressed in a mishmash of clothing and footwear, much of it reportedly donated by climbers from previous expeditions. They moved faster than us carrying loads larger than ours on their heads and backs. Watching them hustle up the trail was humbling.

I saw a tarnished metal sign near the trailhead that designated our route as the "Nalemuru." I asked August as he walked beside me, "Aren't we on the Rongai? What's the Nalemuru?"

"Nalemuru is an old name for this trail. We're on the right one. The old route started at the village of Rongai west of here, but it was closed, and now people call this one the Rongai. Some still call it the Simba," August said, referring to the Swahili word for "lion" made famous by Disney's film "The Lion King."

"Do lions roam here?" I asked, the blood rushing to my face.

"No, not anymore," August assured me. I relaxed.

The path ascended gradually and crested a ridge, reminding me that we weren't on a leisurely stroll. I took in the sound of roots and gravel crackling under my feet and the smell of fresh earth churned by my boots. I enjoyed the sunlight and fresh air after having been cooped up in a stuffy van for hours. The day could not have been better — unless my wife were hiking with me.

We moved out of the woods into a valley filled with fields of highland plants and hearty vegetables. A small village with a handful of small wooden plank houses topped in thatch lay just off the trail. Suddenly, a group of children came running from the settlement and pulled up alongside us. They looked at us with innocent smiles and longing eyes, holding out their hands to accept whatever we wanted to give them. They seemed intent on coaxing candy and whatever goodies they could from us, as if they were versed in the art of shaking down passing trekkers. I fell under their spell and had no choice but to give them some energy snacks. They hung out with us while we had a quick rest break near their home. We smiled and greeted them with "jambo" but kept a close eye on our belongings.

We bid the children goodbye and continued on our way, leaving the farmland for untamed rain forest. We hiked in single file through the woods, chatting and joking as we walked. I demonstrated to Kay and Tom how to smile, drink water through a camelback hose, and wave my arms in the air at the same time without stopping. They laughed and rolled their eyes.

The trail meandered through the trees, around boulders, and over rocks and roots. We encountered several species of monkeys, birds, insects, and lizards on our walking safari. I listened to the sound of the forest and heard voices ahead, where a team of fifty something Germans who looked like veteran mountaineers rested on some logs by the wayside. They were engrossed in lively conversation, and we passed by without a word. They became my personal benchmark. I figured that if I could keep up with them, then I was doing all right. I saw them again up trail as they passed by while we took a rest break. We traded leads for next couple of hours on the way to Camp One.

Hiking lifted my spirits and made me hopeful that I could reach the summit, although the trail was not much more difficult than many others I had done. I knew the route would grow steeper as we approached the final ascent, but for the moment I was optimistic that I stood a good chance of making it safely to the top and back. I had already gone where Harry in *The Snows of Kilimanjaro* had only dreamed. That counted for something.

The trail grew steeper and rockier as it headed up another ridge. Navigating the jagged incline was tricky but manageable without hiking poles. As we ascended from the rain forest into moorland, the trees gave way to a landscape thick with low-lying bushes and shrubs. I saw for the first time since we started our climb a panoramic view of the mountainside and the Serengeti that stretched into Kenya. Gray clouds laden with moisture, rain or snow, drew toward us with impressive speed. August said that we

still had two more hours to go before we reached Camp One. I hoped that we would make it there before the rain came.

An hour later, we stopped for a rest break near another group of climbers. Tom wandered off to take photos while Betty rested. August chatted with his deputy, Minja. Kay and I met two brothers of Lebanese descent who grew up in Tanzania but went to college in the United Kingdom. What a small world, I thought, that an American living in Zambia could meet acquaintances with links to three different countries in the middle of the wilderness. They told us that they climbed Kilimanjaro many times before and were home from London on winter break to give it another go. That's exactly what I wanted do on my vacation, I chuckled, until I realized that I too was spending my break doing the same thing.

We picked our way up the ridge and crossed a wooden bridge straddling a glacier stream. The sound of rushing water as it flowed over the rocky riverbed brought back memories of other encounters with streams or cascading waterfalls I had while hiking. When I asked August if we could stop to enjoy the brook, he pointed uphill and said, "Camp is just up there."

"Great!" I cheered and took off for the campground, leaving the water behind. After more than three hours of hiking, I pulled into a flat clearing where our campsite was pitched. My duffel bag and travel bag sat in a pile of luggage in the middle a circle of tents just off the trail. The entourage of porters and cooks who arrived ahead of us had already set up camp in advance of our arrival. Our dome tents, where we would sleep, and the mess tent, where we would eat, huddled together like a small village, while August's crew camped and cooked in two large tents pitched somewhere in the thicket. I was impressed that the entire support team shared two while I had one myself.

The German climbers and the Tanzanian group arrived in Camp

One at about the same time and carved out their own campsites elsewhere in the clearing. The collective mood in camp was festive with chatter all around about a successful first day of hiking. I spied the other trekkers' digs. Their setups looked nicer than ours with portable tables, camping chairs, and equipment with matching colors and corporate logos. I'm sure that they paid more for those amenities, but for the time being, I didn't mind our no-frills operation. I wondered, though, what else we were missing.

Park rangers manning a small utility shed on the edge of the campground asked all climbers to sign their registry book and guides to present documentation verifying that their groups complied with regulations. August gave the rangers our registration forms and receipt showing that we paid the entrance fee, while the porters weighed their bundles to make sure they weren't overweight. August explained that each porter was allowed to carry up to 15 kilograms (33 pounds). The team came in underweight. Still, it sounded like a lot of weight for anyone to bear, let alone someone ascending a mountain.

Betty, Kay, Tom, and I took turns signing the logbook. I was happy to leave my mark on Kilimanjaro. It was still a long way to the summit, but I reached a personal milestone registering as a climber.

We grabbed our bags and headed to our tents. Betty and Kay went to their double tent, Tom to his, and I to my new home away from home, a small shelter with a waterproof canopy. I pulled my belongings inside like a predator snagging prey, laid out my mattress pad and thermal sleeping bag, changed my clothes, and laid down to rest.

I slept for about an hour before I heard a soft voice call me over and over again to wash up and eat a snack. The words sounded far away, as if I were dreaming, until I opened my eyes and realized that they were coming from someone on August's team. I looked around the tent. The gray interior told me that evening was approaching. Crawling outside, I looked up at the late afternoon sun and saw it fading behind the mountain. The clouds rolled in from the Serengeti bearing rain or snow. A chilly breeze sent me clamoring for my jacket.

I walked away from the campsite toward the latrines. The dark, dingy lair that few dared to use smelled like excrement and was rife with cobwebs. I thought about taking to the bush beyond camp but preferred to brave the toilet over getting caught with my pants down. I survived the outhouse and fled to a bowl of water on a flat rock that served as a makeshift washbasin. Steam wafted up from the warm water into the cold air as the dirt and grime on my hands and face settled in the basin.

Refreshed, I entered the mess tent where Betty, Kay, and Tom were snacking on popcorn, hot tea, and Milo cocoa. Tom made up a fancy recipe for serving Milo that included scoops of mix, sugar, creamer, and hot water. Even in the wilderness, he did it in style.

Betty thought we should acclimatize and suggested that we take an evening stroll up trail. I wanted to rest but reluctantly agreed and hiked with the group for half an hour. I wasn't thrilled at the prospect of doing the same route again the following day but thought it wise to adjust to the height. My chest felt a twinge of tightness that seemed to have been brought on by the hike, but I otherwise felt good. I did not have a headache or other symptoms of altitude sickness. On the trail, I caught my first glimpse of Kibo Peak, Kilimanjaro's summit, rising above the ridgeline. The view must have been like what Harry witnessed when he soared over dark clouds toward heaven. I was heading toward his vision.

We headed back at nightfall when the rain and the temperature began to fall. It was pouring by the time we stumbled into camp. We fled to the mess tent, where the cook served a piping hot dinner that tasted delicious after a long day of cold food. We dined by candlelight and the light of our headlamps on an eclectic meal of bread and jam, cucumber soup, vegetarian pasta, goulash, and mangos. Tom served us on fine aluminum camping dishes with a big smile. "Who wants some gourmet food?"

"I do. It looks delicious," Kay said, peering into the pots of food with a sniff. I said with a disappointed look, "Yeah, but there's no meat."

"You don't need meat! It's fine without it," she laughed with feigned seriousness. She held out a shiny metal plate for Tom to ladle healthy scoops of soup into it. Betty and I did the same. We took turns serving food to each other. I mixed some drinks for Betty and Kay, while Tom jealously guarded his plastic cup of Milo. He really took a liking to the stuff and was determined to fix it just the way he liked it.

"Hey, this soup's not bad," I admitted, savoring the spoonful I tasted. A smile broke on Kay's lips. She said, "Yes, it is. The lasagna's delicious too."

"I think it all tastes pretty good. I have to commend the chef,"

Tom said.

"Me too," Betty chimed in, bundled up and shivering next to the tent door. The thin-walled tent did a poor job of keeping the cold at bay. "It's delicious."

I whined, "Well, just wait until we've been on Kili eating the same food day after day."

It was a special moment eating with friends in a tent on the freezing mountain. A crooked candle made from two candle stubs melted together shed some light but little else. The food and body heat warmed us up. As we dined, the rain picked up and fell in sheets, pelting the tent, but we stayed dry and feasted on our gourmet meal that tasted out of place in our austere surroundings.

When the rain let up, I stumbled out of the mess tent and scrambled in the darkness with my headlamp as a guide. Finding my makeshift home, I dove inside it before the rain picked up again.

I sealed myself inside and crawled into my sleeping bag separated from the cold floor by the thin mattress pad. In for the rest of the night, I set about preparing for the next day's trek. I pulled out a few layers of clothing and set them aside to wear. I decided to wear tennis shoes again after August confirmed that they had sufficient tread to hike the trail to Camp Two. I wanted to put off wearing my heavy hiking boots as long as I could.

I was alone on the cold mountain as the sky poured down on me, bundled up inside a thin tent that strained to keep out the rain and cold, but I didn't mind. I relished having some time to myself after a long bout of hiking. It was a great time to chronicle the day's events, so I pulled out my e-reader and started to write my journal. The Kindle's cumbersome keyboard forced me to tap each letter one by one, but after an hour I typed something that looked like a respectable summary. I considered bringing my laptop computer on the climb but decided that the risk of losing or ruining it on Kilimanjaro was too high.

When my eyes tired from staring at the monochrome screen under the meager light of my headlamp, I stowed the e-reader away, switched off the light, and slid into my sleeping bag, zipping it snugly around my neck to keep my body heat in and the cold air out. I listened to the heavy rain drone on for hours. Winds buffeted the dome tent as the rain pelted its microfiber exterior. The shelter lost the battle against the elements, and rainwater started to leak inside with a drip that sounded like a ticking clock. My body heat kept me warm, but the cold hit my exposed face so fiercely that I had to submerge myself inside the sleeping bag to thaw my cheeks. I came up for air when claustrophobia set in. Small pools of water gathered in the corners of the downhill side of the tent, and I moved my belongings to the other end to keep them dry.

In spite of the miserable weather, I felt good. I was relieved that

I not only survived the first day of the climb but felt better afterwards. My muscles felt stronger after the hike, and I had plenty of stamina. I breathed freely without coughing. My allergies seemed to be in check, and I didn't use my inhaler the entire day.

My mind was too wound up to fall asleep. Alone with my thoughts, I remembered my family and wondered how they were doing. I thought about life at home, what I left behind there, and what would be waiting for me when I returned. My lengthy to-do list crept into my mind, and I shooed it away. I didn't want to think about it when I was no position to deal with it.

I thought about resigning from the Foreign Service and debated the merits of being a diplomat. The diplomatic corps offered great benefits: good pay, a nice lifestyle, travel opportunities, and the chance to promote foreign policy. At the same time, the job threatened to turn me into someone I was not. It was a stressful profession, and the pressure to perform flawlessly swung like a pendulum with dire consequences for failure; in some cases, even death. A plaque in Washington, D.C. listed the names of the hundreds of diplomats who died in the line of duty. While I was optimistic I would never become a casualty, I had no way of knowing what the Foreign Service had in store for me if I continued.

I only knew what it had done to me. It hardened me, forcing me to second guess every decision I made, to defend every position I held, and to distrust others who did not have my interests in mind. The job changed me for the worse, transforming me from an optimistic, open, and honest fellow into a guarded and defensive individual indoctrinated into following orders without regard for my own conscience. It was time for me to reclaim my life and return to who I once was.

Glimpses of my former self reemerged on Kilimanjaro. The mountain stripped away the pretense and trappings of being a diplomat and reduced me to a humble climber. I could use all the capabilities in my arsenal to reach the summit without worrying if I overstepped. I wasn't a natural trekker, but I had strengths I could draw on to succeed. I no longer had to be prim and proper, to impress or kowtow, or put on fake airs in order to make something happen. If I made it past this obstacle, it would be on my own terms. Like Harry Street, I could let go and soar. All I needed to do was rediscover the down-to-earth and unpretentious person that I had once been before the Foreign Service, someone who had an indomitable faith that anything was possible and did it.

I ended the night with a prayer and drifted off to sleep.

7. A Tough Climb to Camp Two

December 28, 2010

I woke up and fell back to sleep several times during the night as I struggled to turn my body inside the sleeping bag. The downpour continued all night long, until it diminished to a drizzle in the early morning. I dreaded the prospect of hiking in the rain, but the weather granted us a reprieve. I opened the tent flap and peered into the clearing to survey the damage. The ground looked damp and muddy but not as messy as I expected after such a drenching. Rain droplets dripped from the trees and beaded up on the waterproof tents. I avoided a pool of water gathered in one corner of the floor and put on my shoes, grabbed my toiletries, and eased my body through the narrow opening without tripping or falling into the mud. Getting out of the small tent was as difficult as doing the limbo.

Mud stuck to my shoes as I clopped over to the latrine. The rain stirred up something so foul in its bowels that the stench almost overwhelmed me like a noxious gas. Given that my only alternative was to head to the bushes in broad daylight, I held my nose and worked as fast as I could without passing out from the smell. Relieved, I lumbered over to the water basin to wash up. Fishing a razor and a small bottle of shaving cream from my carrying case, I lathered my face for a shave.

Just then, Kay popped out of her tent, took a look at my Santa-like beard, and exclaimed, "What in the world are you doing? You don't need to shave up here! We're on a mountain."

I let out a jolly laugh. "I want to look good! I want to be comfortable, not scruffy."

"You think you're uncomfortable? Our tent flooded last night! You have no idea."

I stopped in mid-shave and looked at her, wide eyed. "What?"

"They put the darn tent right in the middle of where the water ran off during the rain. It leaked so much water that all our bags got wet. All our things are soaked!"

"Oh, no!" I gasped as foam dripped from my face.

"Oh, yes. I'm going to talk to August. This is totally unacceptable." Kay stormed off to give our guide an earful. Betty trundled out of the soggy tent and chuckled as she snapped a photo of me with my cream-smeared face. She repeated Kay's lament as I finished shaving, and I gave her my sincere condolences. I splashed cool water on my face and rubbed my hand against my smooth skin, enjoying what was probably the last shave I would have on the climb.

I met Betty and Tom in the mess tent for a quick breakfast. Kay joined us a few minutes later. Betty asked, "Did you talk to August?"

"Yes, I did," Kay answered. "He said they'll be sure to put it up on higher ground tonight."

I wondered it if would rain again at the next camp but held my tongue. Kay and Betty already looked perturbed enough. I ate some porridge with milk and sugar, bread with peanut butter and jam, and some fruit. I noticed that Kay wasn't eating and asked her, "Aren't you going to have something for breakfast?"

"I already ate." The conversation fell silent. August popped his head in the tent and announced in his soothing voice, "It's getting late. We should leave soon. We have a long day of hiking ahead."

We scrambled to finish our meal, stuffing food in our mouths and emptying our plastic drink mugs. Betty and August left straight away while I rushed to change my clothes and pack my bags. Kay and Tom waited for me. My shaving episode held us back.

We left Camp One with the deputy guide, Minja. Our goal was to reach Camp Two, also known as Camp Second Cave, by late afternoon. We had to trek about 12 kilometers (seven miles) and ascend more than 1,000 meters (3,300 feet) to our destination 3,450 meters (11,300 feet) above sea level. August warned us that this hike would be more difficult than the last. This news — or perhaps something I ate for breakfast — left me with a knot in my stomach.

We set out in partly cloudy weather into a light, clinging mist. The cool and fresh morning air offset the body heat I shed from hiking. I felt better when my muscles loosened up, enabling me to move faster. Not far up the trail, we passed August and Betty, who seemed content to take her time. Kay and I pressed on with Minja while Tom stayed back with the others.

An hour later, the clouds parted and the sun appeared, casting a vibrant glow across the landscape that glistened off drops of moisture that clung to the plants and trees. I stopped to put on some waterproof sunscreen, but the sun was so intense that my sweat washed away the cream as fast as I could apply it. I didn't notice until the burn on my face felt hot to the touch. I was grateful when the clouds rolled in again and gave my face a reprieve.

The trail snaked its way up the narrow gully until it disappeared from view. I redoubled my efforts and powered up the hill as quickly as I could, slowing down when I reached the top of the ridge.

I looked out on the horizon and saw the path descend into a long valley before it turned toward another ridge topped with clouds. It looked half as tall as Kibo Peak, whose snow-streaked summit hovered above the cloud line. My eyes traced the route as it vanished in the distance. The realization hit me that we still had a long road ahead of us and that it would take days to reach the top. For the first time on our trip, the climb felt like one. I reassured myself that I could make it.

We stopped for a short break. Winded, I panted, "We...have...a ways...to go."

"I know," said Kay, who didn't look tired at all. "I think we'll make it just fine."

"Speak for yourself," I huffed.

"Don't worry. Just slow down and don't take those hills so fast. Pace yourself. Pole pole," she said, using the Swahili way of saying "slowly, slowly." Minja smiled.

"I wonder if Thor is out here somewhere," I joked, referring to Kay's fictional love interest. "I'll bet he's coming up the trail right now and will pass us soon."

"Oh, please." Kay rolled her eyes with an 'in your dreams' look.

We set off again and marched into the valley. My shoes thumped the ground, disturbing the soil and rock. The thick alpine forest we were in gave way to hauntingly beautiful moorland covered by grass and shrubs. Scattered trees that looked like birches grew fewer and farther apart the more we hiked. Frequent changes in climate and seasons, from wet to dry and back to wet, warped them into bizarre shapes. Old man's beard with a hint of fluorescence covered the trees in wispy bunches. Rocks poked through the sparse grass and heather, giving the terrain a terrestrial look.

We stopped for a break beside the same creek that we saw near Camp One. I sat on a rock and thought of my wife. I pulled my cell phone out of the daypack and waved it in the air to catch a signal, as if I were holding a lighter aloft at a music concert. The phone caught a weak one from the north toward Kenya. I sent Jing a short text message to let her know that I was doing fine. To my surprise, she responded immediately with a message of her own. *That's great, hon! I am so glad to hear from you. Keep it up. Love you!*

I stared at the screen in shock, and a faint cheer escaped my lips. I texted her back as fast as my thumbs could type. *Thanks, hon! I love you too. Signal is weak, but I will write again when I can. Heading to second camp. Love, ME.*

Jing texted me one more time to wish me luck, and I read it a few times. Her messages were just the encouragement I needed to press on. I could hardly believe that I connected with my wife on the mountain. I almost left my phone at home because I didn't think

I need it, but I was glad I brought it.

We hiked away from the creek toward a second ridge that looked shorter but steeper than the first. The trail headed straight for a shroud of mist and disappeared into the clouds. The steep incline and thin air left me chuffing and coughing. I didn't turn to the inhaler because my breathing was steady, but my weary body told me that I needed to slow down. As the trail wound uphill, I asked my partners to stop every few bends to rest. They stopped and waited for me without a word. Kay hardly looked tired, while Minja hiked as if he were taking a leisurely stroll. What I would have given to have some of their strength, I thought wistfully. I tried to breathe through my nose but abandoned the exercise when the incline steepened. I needed all the oxygen my lungs could muster. Thank goodness the altitude and exertion did not leave me struggling to breathe.

The hour-long, exhausting climb to the top of the ridge frustrated me because I couldn't see the ridgeline and didn't know how far we still had to go. When the clouds thinned, I saw the trail continue uphill a good distance but no crest. I stopped to get my bearings and looked back to see how high we had climbed. The valley unfolded before my eyes, forming a giant green bowl between the first and second ridges. The stream vanished into the thicket. I asked Kay, "Where...where do you think Tom and Betty are?"

"I don't know," she said, stopping just ahead of me.

"Oh, there they are," I said, pointing to a gully where a tiny dot of bright orange, Betty's outer vest, bounced on the trail. In their earth tone gear, August and Tom were but barely visible.

"They still have a ways to go," Kay said.

"We have a ways to go too," I said. My eyes followed the path as it snaked up the ridge and disappeared into the clouds. We started climbing again. The temperature plummeted when we entered a thick fog bank. The mist turned to a drizzle mixed with light snow. Shivering, I stopped to put on the inner liner of my jacket and a pair of gloves. Body heat no longer kept me warm. My frozen breath lingered in the air like an apparition. I sighed, "We paid for this?"

"Yes, we did," Kay said wryly as she hiked just ahead of me. She looked as tired of trekking as I, although she seemed to handle the trail much better. The slope continued upward past the point where I thought it should crest. I wondered whether this part of the route was one of the more difficult ones we would face or if the climb would become progressively more difficult. Convinced that the end was near, I set my sights on the invisible ridgeline and imagined myself hiking over it. I wondered how many ridges I needed to pass before I reached the summit.

I looked ahead and spotted a twisted rock formation that materialized through the misty rain. We had not had a break for a while, so I pointed to it and begged Kay, "Can we stop there?"

"Okay," she answered without hesitation. She climbed with stoic resolve, but I could see it slipping. I pressed ahead and reached the outcropping with some difficulty but was rewarded with a view of the elusive ridgeline. I cheered, "Yes! There it is! We're almost to the top."

"Finally! It's about time," she said. We stumbled into a small clearing cradled by the rock formation. I wondered if we should have kept going since that we were close to the ridge but thought it better to take a break. Camp Two could have been near or far for all I knew. "Let's rest here and have a snack."

Kay and I sat on some cold rocks while Minja waited quietly on a decaying log. The rain and snow chilled my skin after I stopped moving, forcing me to put on the knit stocking cap and thermal shirt. We dined on a smorgasbord of snacks to give us energy for the final push to camp. Kay laid out a spread of dried fruit, nuts, sugar chews, and some sweet goop that looked like chocolate snot. She offered me a few. I teased, "Goodness, you look like a pusher."

She laughed. "These were great when I was running marathons. They're really convenient and taste delicious. I remember one time when I was exhausted, I ate some goo and finished the race. You really should try some."

"Don't mind if I do, thanks." I chomped on a sugar chew and squeezed some goop into my mouth. My fat-prone body would have never forgiven me for injecting it with high-calorie substances if I weren't on this mountain. I thanked Kay with a granola bar that seemed mundane compared to the wallop that her magic foods packed.

"Minja, how much longer do we have until we get to Camp Two?" Kay asked our guide. He heard his name and turned his head but did not answer. She rephrased her question. "How far do we have to go to camp? How much time do we have left?"

He said nothing, stood up, and walked over to us. I tapped on my watch and asked, "Minja, how long? How far?"

"Twelve hours," he said. Kay and I looked at each other. He could not have heard us right. There was no way that we had half a day left to hike. I asked in broken English, pointing in the direction of Camp Two, "What time...camp?"

"Twenty-five minutes." That sounded more like it, but he left me confused. We had somewhere between 25 minutes and 12 hours left to go. I wasn't sure if he understood our question. Minja was a good guide but not very helpful when we needed information. He didn't speak English, we didn't speak Swahili, and communicating with hand gestures only got us so far. Kay tried again. "So, we'll be at camp in 25 minutes?"

"Fifteen." We gave up, exasperated. I wished then that I learned some Swahili. My meager vocabulary was limited to "jambo," "pole pole," and "hakuna matata," which wasn't useful on Kilimanjaro unless I wanted a laugh. A few practical Swahili phrases would have helped me communicate with August's team.

Kay and I rested half an hour and were finishing our makeshift picnic when Betty, Tom, and August caught up with us. They arrived as the weather turned even colder. I cheered them on as they made their way to the clearing and pulled up with big smiles on their faces. "Good job! Glad you made it. How are you feeling?"

"Pretty good," Tom smiled, wiping the sweat off his brow.

"I'm tired," Betty gasped. August followed behind with her daypack in hand. I asked, "August, how long will it take until we get to Camp Two?"

"About fifteen minutes." That settled it.

We set off together for the campground. Beyond the second ridge, we hiked through a shallow gully and above the cloud cover into a band of open sky that exposed the rocky, alpine terrain. The view of the horizon above the clouds at 3,500 meters (11,500 feet) was spectacular.

We climbed out of the trough and headed uphill toward the final ridge standing in the way of Camp Two. August took us on a short detour to a cave underneath an arch of rock large enough to fit a small house. We loitered a few minutes before the cold sent us fleeing back to the trail.

The final ridge was easier to scale than the previous one. Knowing that our destination lay on the other side, I walked with a spring in my step, hopscotching from stone to stone to avoid stepping in mud. We split up to move at our own pace. Kay went on ahead while Tom and Betty lingered behind. I hiked alone.

The scramble to the ridgeline was the steepest yet. My gloved hands and willpower propelled me to the crest. My breathing grew labored and my heart fluttered, fanning my concern that I was pushing myself too hard. I cleared the final rock outcropping and hustled to the top. Camp Two appeared below me like Shangri-la in a depression encircled by crumbling hills and a large cave carved into the hillside. The settlement, with its pitched tents, picnic tables and scattered latrines, beckoned. I exhaled a sigh of relief. I survived another day's trek. It was exhilarating getting past the most difficult hike I'd done in years, although I knew it was only a warm-up for what lay ahead.

I picked my way into camp and found our campsite among the dozen scattered around the bowl. The tents were pitched with our bags laid out neatly beside them. I washed up at an outdoor faucet fed by glacier water before rendezvousing with the others for lunch. The carrot soup, curry fries, coleslaw, and fruit did not seem quite as gourmet as they had the previous night, but I had nothing to complain about because the cooks could only serve whatever they carried up the mountain.

Awake and feeling invigorated, I wandered around the encampment after lunch. The number of climbers at Camp Two seemed to have doubled from the day before. August explained that some groups hiked from the Rongai trailhead to Camp Two in just one day. The campground looked more hospitable than the first one. Clean latrines that did not stink and a fresh bucket of water to wash hands did wonders for the ambiance.

I walked over to the outhouses and met an older German mountaineer named Rolf. A jovial sort, he launched without a word from me into stories about trekking in the Alps and an earlier Kilimanjaro climb. This trip was his requiem; something he wanted to do before he grew too old. Puffing on a cigarette, waving it in the air like a baton, he said in a thick Bavarian accent, "Ja, I know I should not smoke, but like it. I climb mountains all the time. No problem for me."

"By all means! Don't let me stop you," I said, smiling. "It was a pleasure meeting you, Rolf. Good luck with your climb and getting into the toilet!"

He nodded his head as I gave up on the latrine and walked away. I went over to look at the cave — presumably Second Cave — at the edge of camp. It was big enough to hold several tents, but the park authorities banned teams from camping in it out of concern that it would collapse. I doubted that was going to happen anytime soon. It had already stood for millennia and would probably still be there after we were long gone. Someone placed a bleached water buffalo skull at the entrance, as if warning that anyone caught sleeping there would suffer the same fate.

I snoozed most of the afternoon. Feeling rested, I slithered out of my tent and stumbled into an incredibly majestic view of the Kilimanjaro summit. The clouds parted and the sun appeared, brightening the landscape and warming the air. Kibo Peak rose high in all its glory, as if to say that only those who were worthy could behold her full beauty. Lacey folds of snow lay gently in crevasses made by long-vanished glaciers that raked the mountainside. I was mesmerized by the amazing view and gazed at it for what seemed an eternity. At that moment, there was nowhere else on Earth I wanted to be.

I spotted the others making their way back to camp, presumably from an acclimatization hike. They descended the ridge and headed my way.

"Hey guys, the view is incredible! Let's take a photo!" I hollered and waved at them. Betty, Kay, and Tom joined me for a group photo with August behind the lens. The ridge sheltering Camp Two briefly kept the clouds at bay. Looking out over the Serengeti, I saw the flank where we climbed earlier in the day fade into the mist.

Fifteen minutes later, the clouds rolled in and Kibo Peak disappeared. The temperature dropped to a freezing chill. The rain returned, and we hastened to the mess tent for a hodgepodge dinner of soup, pasta, and something that looked like chunky sauce.

"Darn, no meat again," I lamented.

"Well, I think the dinner's good," Kay said. "I like the soup."

"It's okay," Betty said. She didn't eat much.

"I wonder if there's any of that goulash left," Tom said.

"I doubt it," Kay answered. "I think the cooks ate the leftovers."

"If you need some meat, Tom, I have an emergency can of Spam in case of meat withdrawals," I said. "Want some?"

"No, thank you," he said, whipping up a cup of Milo cocoa like an archeologist unearthing a treasured find. He held up his concoction and took a sip. "Ah."

The heavy rain and hints of fatigue dampened my enthusiasm for dinner. It did not look appealing at all. I thought about fetching the Spam but did not want to go back to my tent to retrieve it. The rain turned into a downpour. I asked Betty and Kay, "Is your tent in a good spot tonight? I hope you won't be flooded again."

"I think so," Betty said, "My clothes still aren't dry from last night's soaking."

"I sure hope so," Kay answered. "I don't want to go through that again!"

"Definitely not!" Tom said.

We finished eating and raced to our tents when the rain started to fall in unrelenting waves. I was soaked by the time I covered the short distance from the mess tent to mine. Sealing myself inside my shelter, I ripped off my wet clothing and muddy boots, laid them out to dry in a corner, and donned some warm, dry clothing before I froze. I deferred clean up until the morning.

My bottled water depleted, I resorted to drinking boiled glacier water. My tent became a laboratory for making drink concoctions. I added flavored drink mix to mask the gritty taste of silt, but the experiment went horribly wrong when I spilled some of the cherry-flavored powder on my fingers and stained them blood red. I managed to fill the bottles with the ruby liquid, but cleaning up my mess without staining my gear was maddeningly frustrating.

I hopped into my sleeping bag and listened to the sound of rain reverberate on the tent walls. The night was young, and I was still lucid after napping. I pulled out the Kindle and wrote in my journal for a while until switching to *The Snows of Kilimanjaro*. I empathized with Harry, the Hemingway character some say reflected the author himself, who suffered a terrible death in the shadow of the very peak I was climbing. I was not far from the leopard carcass that Harry envisioned in his dream. I wondered whether I could avoid his fate and find a new life on the other side of this deadly mountain. I prayed that I would succeed where he had failed.

I finished reading and listened to a mix of songs on my iPod music player, losing myself in the melody. The screen emitted a glow that brightened the dark tent. As the songs played, my mind drifted on a spiritual journey. I was consumed by myriad thoughts. I remembered my family and wished that they were with me. I thought about my wife camping in this place. I recalled how she bravely summited Kilimanjaro and wondered whether I could too.

With music playing softly in my ears, I drifted off into a deep sleep. I did not dream, perhaps because my experience on Kilimanjaro was so unreal that it had to be an illusion.

8. Hiking into the Clouds

December 29, 2010

The rain ended in the early morning. I poked my head outside and saw rays of beautiful sunshine wash over the waterlogged campground. The deep blue sky was a godsend after two nights of heavy rain. The temperature was cool but not freezing; the air smelled fresh. Water left over from the deluge flowed downhill or evaporated in the sun. I pulled back the tent flap and inched my way outside, careful not to touch the muddy tarp at the entrance. I put on my hiking boots to walk around camp. They were still clean but would look muddy and broken in soon enough.

I stood up and paced about the campsite to work out the kinks in my muscles. My entire body felt sore and tight after two days of hiking, my legs most of all. Sleeping overnight on the hard ground with nothing but a thin mattress pad and sleeping bag, compounded by the pounding I took on the trail, left me feeling drained. I picked my way through the mud and pools of draining water to a nearby clearing where I could stretch. I was never one to condition my muscles before and after exercising, but I needed to break that bad habit in order to give myself a fighting chance on Kilimanjaro. The mountain would punish me if I stretched my body to the limits without limbering up. I resolved to work my arms, torso, and legs every morning as long as I was still standing.

Kibo Peak reached for the sky yet looked close to the touch, and it beckoned me to head for the summit, a temptation that flattered me with a false confidence. I could not have chosen a better relief for my morning stretch. I faced the mountain and stretched in ways that made me look as if I were performing a sacred rite. I bowed and prostrated my body like a supplicant in a traditional ceremony, casting my arms and legs about in an elaborate ritual. The sunlight painted the landscape in surreal colors. The rock was more brilliant and the shadows deeper and more pronounced in the sunlight. I turned around in mid-exercise and beheld the Serengeti unfurling for miles across the plains into Kenya. Some claimed that Mount Kilimanjaro offered the best views in the world. Looking down on the world below, I had to agree.

I finished my stretching, walked back to the campsite, and ran into the animated figures of Betty and Kay, who were apparently upset. I made the mistake of opening my mouth. "Good morning! How are you?"

"Our tent was flooded again! Everything is soaked!" Betty answered with fiery eyes, tossing her wet clothes on every available surface to dry them in the sunlight.

"Two nights in a row!" growled Kay. "This is totally unacceptable. We have to dry all of our clothing again!"

I looked around and saw rivulets of rainwater draining into pools of standing water under their tent. It lay right in the path of what turned overnight into a glacier stream. My hearty domicile was again spared the worst of the onslaught. The inside was cold, uncomfortable, and austere, but at least it kept me dry. Poor Betty and Kay were washed out two nights in row. I couldn't complain.

The situation could have been worse. Rain inundated Camp Two for three straight days when Jing's group passed through the area, but I didn't have the gumption to tell that to the ladies. While they had the misfortune of sleeping in places hit by run-off, the climb had otherwise gone well. I thought we were fortunate. Our circumstances could have changed at any moment; we had no way to know what lay in store for us in this unpredictable environment where fate moved like the wind.

August told us at breakfast that we needed to trek another 500 vertical meters to Camp Three, or Camp Third Cave, located at 3,850 meters (12,650 feet). The trail we were going to take deviated from the main branch of the Rongai Route, which veered southwest to Mawenzi Tarn Camp. We planned to head southeast and reunite with the main route at Kibo Huts, the summit base camp. Our guide reassured us that this hike would be easier and the slope more gradual, aside from a steep ascent at the outset. He advised us that the first ridge was steep and muddy enough that we would need hiking poles to give us leverage and prevent slippage. I grabbed the sturdy poles that I inherited from Jing. Little did I know how essential they would become.

Although the first ridge did not look difficult as I departed, I struggled to climb it. My boots slipped repeatedly on the wet rock, stirring up small avalanches of dirt and gravel that cascaded downhill. The hiking poles caught me from sliding a couple times. I didn't need crampons to scale the ridge but wished the soles of my new hiking boots had better traction. A stream of porters and cooks who had stayed behind to tear down our campsite caught up with me and breezed by wearing loafers and tennis shoes and carrying baskets and bags. I shook my head in disbelief. Turning my attention to the ridgeline, I pressed on. Kay and Tom, with Minja in the lead, made it to the top and waited for me. I pulled myself up a few minutes later and sighed with relief that the most difficult portion of the day's hike was behind me. Betty struggled with the ridge, and August stayed with her. Kay, Tom and I went on ahead with Minja and Manda, another guide who doubled as a porter.

The slope moderated with a slight incline that stretched into the distance and disappeared into the mist. The ethereal sunshine that I basked in at camp vanished behind a cloud bank that shrouded the earth in a soft white mist. The fog descended and covered the land in shadows. The temperature fell, prompting me to don my jacket, gloves and stocking cap. The cloud cover ebbed and flowed as if it were breathing, sometimes pulling back to reveal the path ahead before concealing it again. The group spread out and hiked quietly in a long line. The loose gravel echoed under my feet, intensified by the silence in the air. I was too fascinated by the landscape to say a word.

We moved through desolate ravines formed by lava flows, shaped by now-extinct glaciers. Rock sentries warped by millennia of erosion stood at attention along the trail like landmarks guiding us through the fog. We passed from the heath-filled moorlands into the mountain's desert zone. With terrain devoid of trees, sparse vegetation beyond flowering sagebrush and moss, and rolling mist that mixed with rain, the landscape conjured images of the Scottish highlands. The occasional porter who passed by with a large bag on his head reminded me that we were a long way from there.

I could not think of a landscape more frigid or alien on a continent better known for its tropical forests and savannas. Kilimanjaro lay in Africa's Afromontane region, an area straddling the Equator with clusters of freestanding mountains and plateaus surrounded by lowlands. This was an exotic volcano unlike any on Earth, with climate zones ranging from tropics and savannas to moorlands, tundra and desert. A sky island more at home in the far reaches of the northern and southern hemispheres than the equatorial tropics, Kilimanjaro featured amazing biodiversity.

Although I did not see the frozen leopard in Harry's dream, I was surprised to find that so much wildlife ranged at this altitude. White-necked black ravens circled campgrounds scavenging for food discarded by humans. Small lizards crossed my path. They had no need to worry about predators, but I wasn't sure how the cold-blooded creatures stayed warm enough to survive the low temperatures or what they ate since so few insects, flies or mosquitos, lived this high. Why any creature would live high on the mountain when better climes lay in the lowlands I had no idea — one week up here was enough for me.

I fished the iPod from my daypack and turned on a music medley to accompany me on the trail. Thank goodness that Steve Jobs had the vision to make a portable jukebox capable of storing thousands of songs. The music offered a melodic diversion from the muted sounds of Kilimanjaro; the ever-changing landscape and dancing clouds became my video. My boots toe tapped to the beat on the rocky path, my hiking poles became a makeshift air guitar, and my booty began to shake. I crossed the line when I belted out my own rendition of the Billy Ray Cyrus song "Achy Breaky Heart" and wound up driving Kay and Tom to distraction. I quit after the second stanza when they jokingly warned me that they were going to throw me off the mountain if I continued. Perhaps I would have gotten a better reception if I sang his daughter Miley Cyrus' song "The Climb."

We stopped for a rest midway to camp but did not linger long because of the cold. Minja and Manda took off their oversized backpacks and sat down on nearby boulders. Kay, Tom, and I huddled together to keep warm. Leaning on my poles, I looked around and remarked, "It's pretty desolate, don't you think?"

"Yeah, it looks like the moon," Tom answered. "We're a long way from home."

"I like the landscape. It's really beautiful," Kay said, "It looks like another world."

"You can see the remains from old lava flows. This must have been quite a volcano at one time," I added, pointing toward an outcropping. "The mountain's massive. I can't imagine what it was like when it was active."

"Yep," Tom nodded, taking a swig of his flavored drink.

"It's getting cold," Kay said. She was wearing a tank top, apparently unfazed by the chill, while I was bundled up. "I was just getting warmed up. Let's get going soon before I get cold."

We nodded and snapped a few photos before heading out on our final push to Camp Three.

The fog set in and made it difficult for us to locate the trail. Minja took the lead and guided us to make sure we stayed on track. The chilly air blew against my face, and I pressed my gloved hands against my cheeks to warm them. Heavy clothing trapped my body heat. The alien landscape, what little I could make out, looked like a scene from another world deformed by the once-heavy volcanic activity that left behind odd lava formations and debris. We marched for more than an hour through a field of rust-tinged rocks that looked like the surface of Mars.

The clouds thinned, and a campground appeared just ahead in a large glacier-carved valley. We were almost to Camp Three. Also known as Camp Third Cave, the site derived its name from the porous caves adorning rock walls that surrounded the encampment and sheltered it from the heavy winds that blew down from Kibo Peak. The place was unusually calm for an area often buffeted by winds.

Kay, Tom and I arrived at the campground with our guides in less than three hours, sooner than expected for a short hike. Betty followed with August an hour later. I was relieved how easy this trek was compared to what we went through the day before. I felt good. I was in the best shape I'd been in weeks just a couple days away from my summit attempt. My breathing was stable, and I didn't feel a smidgeon of altitude sickness. Still, I knew that my body needed to rest up for the bigger challenge ahead.

Sunlight filtered through the clouds and warmed the camp

enough for us to wait outside until the porters set up the tents. I wanted to camp inside one of the caves, sheltered from the elements, but a posted sign warned, "Sleeping in caves has been prohibited. Please use tents." What I would have given to stay there!

Betty, Kay, and I chatted while Tom wandered around trying to find a phone signal. He looked lost and distracted as he moved in haphazard circles and waved his phone in the air. Betty complained, "I have got to get my damp clothes dry! They're still soaked from this morning. It's probably too cold for them to dry here."

"Give it a try," I suggested. "Even if they freeze, you'll get out some of the moisture."

"Okay, but I doubt it. My clothes have been wet this whole trip. Now they're going to be cold and stiff as a board."

"Mine too. It better not rain again tonight," Kay added. At this altitude, any precipitation was likely to fall as snow.

"I'm really sorry you've both had such bad luck with the flooding, but I don't think it will happen again tonight," I tried to reassure them. Pointing to the porters who were digging drainage trenches around their tent to divert water away from it, I said, "It looks like August is making sure your tent will stay dry if it rains. I don't think it will flood anyway. It's too cold."

"I hope not," Kay said. "One more time…"

At that moment, Tom wandered back, staring at his phone. I asked, "Did you get a signal?"

"Yes, I did," he responded, pointing away from our campsite. "It seems to be better over there near that rock."

"Great!" I exclaimed and grabbed my daypack. "I'm going to write to Jing."

I walked over to where Tom pointed and tapped a message on

my smartphone. *Hon, I made it to third camp. Half way to the summit. I feel good. Miss you lots. Love, ME.*

The phone caught a signal, and the message transmitted. I waited for a few minutes to see if my wife would write back but didn't hear from her. I knew she was heading to Livingstone, Zambia to spend New Year's weekend at Victoria Falls with her parents and our son and would write me when she could. Sending her daily updates on our progress and getting responses from her was one of my biggest thrills on this trip. It as if I was on the battlefield craving letters from home.

August was chatting with the others when I returned to the campsite. He said, "Tomorrow we will go on an acclimatization hike half way to the top of Kibo Peak and then come back here. This will help minimize the effects of altitude sickness."

"How long will it take?" Tom asked.

"About five hours," August said. "Remember that you may have headaches, lightheadedness and lost appetite. The altitude here is high. Please be careful."

I heard an edge in his voice. I knew from experience that altitude sickness could hit at any time, unexpectedly, like when I suddenly fell ill high in the Andes Mountains of South America during a visit to La Paz, Bolivia. I dreaded the thought of being revisited by a splitting headache, upset stomach, nausea, vomiting, weakness, and chills. I could not imagine making it to the top of Kilimanjaro in that condition. This was the last day I could start taking Diamox before the summit attempt and have some measure of protection. I decided not to use it and hoped that I wouldn't regret my choice. I still felt fine even though I was well above the threshold for succumbing to altitude sickness; I felt better than I had in the lowlands of Zambia. I did not want to resort to taking Diamox needlessly and lose my appetite or worse.

I spent the afternoon in my tent napping and jamming to music. Rested, I joined Kay, Tom and Minja before nightfall for a short hike. Betty stayed behind to recuperate. Dark clouds gathered on the horizon, so I put on my waterproof poncho as a precaution and hoped it would not start raining while we were outdoors. We had been blessed with terrific weather on this trip, but I knew from the flooding in the first two campgrounds that storms could hit us at any time.

As we set off from Camp Three on the trail heading to Kibo Huts, I felt the heavy atmosphere put pressure on my lungs and hamper my breathing. The climb wasn't difficult — the slope rose gradually, and we hiked at a leisurely pace — but the air's reduced oxygen content left me more winded than I would have been at a lower altitude. The pressure was palpable, and I remembered to move slowly to adjust to the reduced oxygen levels. So this was what it was like to suffer from a slow asphyxiation, I thought.

The rain stopped and the clouds drifted away, revealing the stunningly beautiful gorge we were hiking. Kibo Peak materialized to my right, and to my left, the majestically jagged and snow-capped Mount Mawenzi reached for the sky. The barren, U-shaped gorge cascaded from the flanks of Kibo Peak and spilled down toward the lowlands as far as the eye could see. It looked like an ancient thoroughfare created by the lava that once flowed from the extinct volcano and by the vanished glaciers that followed. Far out on the Serengeti, I saw the twinkle of lights from towns dotting the plains. The fantastic sight would have made a wonderful setting for a fantasy novel. I imagined the Misty Mountains in J.R.R. Tolkien's Middle Earth. That this alpine tundra lay in the heart of Africa astounded me.

Kay, Tom, and I hiked for an hour to a vista high above Camp Three while Minja shadowed us. Scanning the horizon, I saw dozens of manmade rock piles dotting the landscape. Some were simple, others more complex. August said that they were trail markers, but many showed a symmetry and elegance that suggested they were constructed to commemorate a climb, remember a loved one, or just for fun. I wanted to make one for Jing to memorialize her ascent but opted not to because I didn't want to keep the others waiting while I built one.

We returned to the campground before dark. I stopped by the rock where I earlier picked up a cell phone signal and checked my phone for a message from my wife. Powering it on, I waited anxiously to see if text would pop up. Sure enough, it did. I scanned the bright screen in the dim light. *Hon, I am glad you made it and feel good. I am proud of you. I love your messages. Everyone says hello. Miss you very much!*

I was ecstatic to hear from Jing. Her message capped off a wonderful day. Her words encouraged me and made me feel as if she were hiking with me. At the same time, they made me miss my family all the more. I would see them soon enough, whether I reached the summit or not. Sharing moments like these with my wife was priceless.

I headed to the mess tent for dinner in good spirits. Betty was inside sipping tea, cupping the mug in her gloved hands to keep warm. The temperature dropped to freezing after the sun disappeared behind the mountain. Kay and Tom joined us, and we sat on the floor, each one in a corner, shivering to keep warm. The interior thawed from the body heat and frozen breaths, the flicker of candlelight and headlamps, and the friction from our winter gear. The thin blanket on the floor did little to protect our bums from the cold that seeped up from the ground.

"Soup, again?" Tom asked in an exaggerated voice as he fixed himself a hot cup of Milo. "I can't wait to have a taste."

We chuckled and nodded. Even the vegetarians in our group, Betty and Kay, seemed to tire of the same uninspiring fare. The dinner was very similar to the ones we had eaten over the past two days. Try as he might, the cook could only prepare a limited variety of vegetable soup and dishes with pasta and sauce pleasing to our palettes. In spite of the cold and monotonous cuisine, the mood was upbeat. There was nothing like an uneventful hike to make a good day on the mountain even better.

Tom said, "I thought today went very well, but I'm sure it's not going to get any easier."

"It was good, wasn't it?" I said. "I had a little trouble on that first ridge, but after that it was smooth sailing."

"I did too," Betty agreed. "I feel better now than last time. This gives me hope that I'll get to the top this time."

"Definitely," I said. "I wonder if what we've done is anything like we're going to go through on the summit."

"I doubt it," Tom said. "The summit's going to be much harder."

"Thanks for the confidence boost," I grinned.

"My pleasure!"

Betty chimed in. "Tom's right. It's much harder. The mountain face is really steep. I got to the rim at Gilman's Point but couldn't go any further because I was so sick. I went blind too. I couldn't see! My vision was horrible. The guides almost had to carry me down."

I almost choked on a spoonful of soup as I digested her sobering words. Changing the subject, I asked, "What are we doing here freezing in this tent when we could be with our families? Are we crazy?"

"Maybe a little bit," Tom smiled. I thought I saw a glimpse of the wild-eyed adventurer.

Kay smiled. "Definitely."

At nightfall the chill came with a vengeance. We wrapped up our meal when the temperature inside the tent plunged and frost began to creep in, robbing us of heat. Shivering, I left the mess tent and headed to the latrine before making my way to my tent. The crescent moon and an array of stars blossomed in the night sky and illuminated the landscape with twinkles of light that danced on the thick layer of frost covering every surface. I looked up and saw the Southern Cross hanging in the sky. The heavens were bright enough that I did not need a headlamp to pick my way around tents and boulders. I could have gazed upward forever, but the bitter cold sent me seeking shelter.

I sealed my tent as tightly as I could, wrapped myself in four layers of clothing and the outer lining of my jacket, and threw the rest of my gear under my mattress pad to add extra layers between the freezing ground and me. Preparations for the next day's hike had to wait until morning. I slipped into my sleeping bag and zipped it over my head, leaving a small opening to let the air circulate. The cold played with my emotions. It made me want to be off the mountain and resting at home in my own bed. It encouraged me to quit the climb while I was ahead and give up this silly idea that climbing a mountain could lead to a new life. Wallowing in self-pity, I found myself leery of the future and clinging to the past. Fighting my doubts, I told myself to stay the course, face this challenge, and conquer it. The tension warmed the air, making it almost bearable.

I spent the evening inside my sleeping bag listening to music and writing. I wondered whether I was the first person to use a Kindle on Kilimanjaro to chronicle their climb as it happened. The glow from the e-reader and the iPod screen lit up the bedroll like a lantern in a cave. I thought it ironic that these innovations made life more entertaining but did not make it more comfortable. These tech gadgets did little to make climbing Mount Kilimanjaro any easier.

I thought about the team. This was the point in our trip when the environment affected our attitudes and messed with our physical and emotional well-being. Our idiosyncrasies were going to emerge and potentially affect our personal relationships. Two nights of flooding had certainly affected Betty and Kay. Betty complained more and demanded more from our guide. Kay grew testy when it came to our accommodations. Tom was doing fine, but who knew what lay ahead. I enjoyed getting to know them all. They were people with whom I could commiserate and from whom

I drew inspiration. I was glad that we avoided the drama that happened so often in groups with relationship issues. The four of us got along as well as could have been expected given that we spent every moment awake together with nothing more than sponge baths.

I powered down my electronics and settled in for the evening, but sleep eluded me. I lay motionless so I didn't have to fight with my sleeping bag. I listened to the workers in a nearby tent chatting in Swahili. Their loud voices resonated in the cold air. They talked and laughed late into the night, keeping me awake for hours. They jabbered on about things that seemed light years away from me. I had no idea what they said but imagined that they were talking about whatever concerned guides, porters, and cooks working on Kilimanjaro.

I wished that I knew some Swahili so I could talk to the men who supported us. Except for August, we had not gotten to know the support team well because we couldn't communicate with them. They usually kept to themselves when we were in camp and were often out of sight unless we saw them on the trail or working in campsites. I would have liked to have gotten to know them but found myself stuck behind a language barrier.

I admired those who worked on Kilimanjaro. They climbed this mountain up and down, over and over, in any kind of weather, just to help clients fulfill their audacious dream of reaching a place humans were not meant to inhabit. Even though climbers were responsible for getting themselves to the summit, the workers carried most of their belongings and camping gear. I couldn't imagine working in such a hostile environment. The pay was puny by western standards, although the jobs were more lucrative than most on the local economy since the workers earned extra money from tips. Many were obviously passionate about their work and seemed to take pride in being a member of an elite group of individuals, though I imagined that to some it was just a job. August said that most men started out as porters or cooks and became guides after graduating from mountaineering school. Park management hired some graduates to work as rangers. A few, like August, went on to start their own outfitters.

The porters talked on into the night about things unknown. At some point, their voices melded with my dreams, and I drifted into unconsciousness for the rest of the night.

9. Getting Schooled at School Hut

December 30, 2010

"Time to wake up, Mike," I vaguely heard Betty's voice call outside my tent. I came to my senses, extracted my body from the sleeping bag, and answered, "Okay, thanks. I'm awake."

"Good. See you at breakfast," Betty's voice said. The sound of footsteps faded. I wiped my eyes and looked at my watch. The display read 7:15 a.m. Kept awake much too late by chatty workers, I overslept but not late enough to keep the group waiting. I didn't get enough sleep but felt unusually rested. More light than usual filtered through the tent fabric and warmed the interior. I unzipped the flap and peered outside. The sun was too bright for my sleepy eyes, and I shut them until they adjusted to the glare. Sunlight lit up my tent. After last night's deep freeze, the bright morning was a welcome change.

I dressed, grabbed my carrying case, and put on my boots, which were caked with dried mud. I shimmied my way out of the tent and stretched, breathing in the fresh air. The warm sun shone intensely in the clear sky, melting the frost and evaporating the lingering moisture. Majestic Kibo Peak once again towered above the campground. I wanted to do some exercises but wasn't sure how soon the group would leave, so I passed on them. I grabbed my daypack and hiking poles in case I needed to make a quick getaway.

Looking around, I saw Tom exiting the latrine and Betty heading toward it while Kay washed up at the plastic washbasin. I walked toward her. "Good morning, Kay. How did you sleep last night?"

"Much better. Thank goodness it didn't rain. For once our tent isn't flooded," she said with a smile.

"That's good. Glad to hear it. I assume your stuff is dry."

"Yes, it is, thank goodness," she said. "How'd you sleep?"

"Oh, not bad. The workers kept me up for a while, but I slept well."

"I know. They bothered me for a while too. Okay, the water's all yours," she said, wringing her hands and heading to breakfast. I cleaned up and joined her at one of the few picnic tables in the campground, a nice change of scenery from the mess tent. The morning was pleasant enough to dine outside, not wet and nippy as usual. Weather conditions had generally been so good that I was afraid our luck would run out and we would run into rain or snow. I looked up at the cloudless sky and scanned the barren surface of Kibo Peak. Unless inclement weather set in, the trail promised to be dry all the way to the summit.

Breakfast was a repeat of what we ate every morning. I consumed an eclectic meal of fried eggs with cucumbers, tomatoes, toast, and millet porridge with the flavor and consistency of gelatin. I treated myself to Korean coffee, a guilty pleasure I acquired when I lived in South Korea. The mocha-flavored instant coffee packed a jolt of caffeine, sugar, and cocoa that I hoped would give me an energy boost on the trail. It tasted better to me than the generic instant coffee or tea I had been drinking. It almost rivaled the taste of Milo.

August stopped by to share details about the acclimatization hike. We planned to ascend more than 1,300 meters (4,300 feet) from Camp Three to School Hut and back again, a four-hour circuitous route that at the end of the day would put us no closer to the Kilimanjaro summit. The trek was devoted entirely to adjusting to higher altitudes to keep us from getting sick. August encouraged us to depart as soon as possible, his urgent tone telling me that we needed to leave immediately. I gobbled up breakfast, threw my bags together for the porters, and gathered my belongings for the hike.

Kay and I sprinted ahead with our guide, Minja, while Tom and August stayed with Betty, who moved at a slower pace. As I set out on the trail, I felt my heart flutter. I tried to dismiss it as nothing, but memories of my illness crossed my mind. Heart palpitations were good for those in love but not ideal for a climber ready to go vertical. My racing heartbeat settled down after a few minutes of slow hiking. I prayed that it was under control and wouldn't flare up again.

We hiked uphill at a steady pace but were again passed by dozens of overburdened and underdressed porters. Many were from other groups heading to Kibo Huts to prepare their clients for the final ascent. Except for August and Minja, our team stayed at Camp Three awaiting our return. Surely the fact that I could not keep up with the porters while I carried nothing more than a daypack and hiking poles was because I was too busy enjoying the scenery, I thought. I didn't need to keep up with them, I reasoned.

This wasn't a race. I needed to take it slow. *Pole pole*, slowly slowly. Then again, maybe I was just slow.

We followed the same route up the gorge that we hiked the previous night before veering off to another trail that headed straight for Kibo Peak. It passed through a long valley and snaked its way uphill through lava flows toward the summit. The sparse vegetation virtually disappeared, leaving an alpine desert that looked like a lunarscape filled with surreal rock formations. They grew increasingly pronounced the higher we hiked with larger boulders and more twisted outcroppings. The area reminded me of the desolate terrain around Mount St. Helens, another volcano that last erupted in 1981. Unlike St. Helens, Kilimanjaro was long extinct, although I would not have known it from its terrain. I saw signs of volcanic activity everywhere that could have been as old as a century or a millennium.

I looked up and wondered how high we would climb this time. The top of Kibo Peak looked deceptively close, but I did not see any sign of School Hut. Kay and Minja zipped ahead, stopping occasionally to let me catch up, while I took photos. I put on some sunscreen and donned my iPod to let the music distract me. The percussion-heavy, lively song "Good Life" by the band *OneRepublic* became one of my favorite trail songs. The simple melody with its three-tone whistle that reminded me of a Swiss yodel, rising and falling like the mountain, nudged me onward. The memorable sound passed my lips and burrowed itself in my mind.

We pulled up to an outcropping overlooking the valley and stopped for a rest. The line of porters, climbers and guides heading on the trail to Kibo Huts looked like a stream of industrious ants. Gesturing toward the gorge, I piped up, "Hey, look how far we've come. That's amazing! Just a few days ago we were way down there."

"That's true," Kay said, leaning her chin on her hiking poles. "But I can't wait to beat Martina!"

"You're already way ahead of her in my book," I joked. Kay made it her personal mission to climb higher than former tennis star Martina Navratilova, who was evacuated from Kilimanjaro a few weeks before. I said, "I think she turned back somewhere below Kibo Huts. You have nothing to worry about. We're already higher than she got."

Kay chuckled. "Well, I'll know for sure once we reach School Hut. My daughter was worried that I wouldn't make it to the top after she read about what happened to Martina. I'll have to tell her I beat her."

"That's the spirit!" I grinned, taking a drink of cherry-flavored glacier water. That was Kay. One part no nonsense and driven, one part free spirit and lighthearted. We got along well. She inspired me to push myself harder but always followed it up with moral support and energy snacks.

Our frivolity ended when we started to climb switchbacks up Kibo's steep face. The hike was more difficult than our earlier treks. No amount of training short of climbing a mountain could have prepared me for it. Scree on the trail bedeviled my boots as I kicked loose rock and gravel and slid backward with each step. The clouds descended, chilling the air, and the wind picked up, blowing sand in my face with shrill blasts. I was grateful that sunglasses protected my eyes from the gusts. I choked when the dust collected in my lungs and coughed, gasping for air. My chest felt tight with a dull ache that I had not felt since Zambia. Something, perhaps the dust or lack of oxygen, seemed to trigger my allergies and belabor my breathing. I struggled to keep moving and fretted that this would-be acclimatization hike was close to causing a relapse of my illness. Lingering thoughts of how lucky I was to climb Africa's highest mountain disappeared in the blowing sand.

Kay and I slowed our pace and stopped at every turn. Mortality forced both of us to catch our breath and let our muscles rest longer than we would have liked in the middle of the sandstorm. Kay looked tired too but still showed the same resolve she displayed on the way to Camp Two.

We searched for School Hut but to no avail. The place was the halfway point of our hike but also the highest point we would climb before our summit attempt, and I was certain that if I reached it I could handle the rest. We grumbled that the campground always seemed to be "just over the next ridge." A blanket of drab gray clouds covered the landscape with dust, our trail fading into the smog. I vaguely saw the outlines of a few rock formations but not School Hut.

We kept hiking. Each bend became more difficult than the last as the grade steepened. It tested me, but I persevered and inched my way up the mountain, step by agonizing step. I focused on putting one foot in front of the other and taking one step at a time. Stride by stride, footfall by footfall, I moved upward. I stopped and started too many times to count. My body felt weak, and I relied on willpower to keep going. Putting away my music player, which had become a nuisance, I listened to the sound of my boots grinding scree and my hiking poles kicking rocks as they pointed the way to School Hut. My breathing echoed in my ears as each inhale and exhale sounded like air passing through a respirator. I pulled my jacket over my mouth to try to keep dust particles out of my lungs, to little effect.

My eyes scanned the alien landscape for signs of life. As I climbed out of the turbulent clouds into clear skies and calm air, a cluster of buildings sheltered by rim rock materialized in the distance. School Hut! I was so relieved. The sight of it, no matter how far away, gave me hope. I prayed the worst was over. It pained me to stop to rest and hike slowly with our destination in sight, but I thought it better to play it cautious than to use up my remaining strength bolting over to it. I still needed to get back to Camp Three.

I grew irritated at August for insisting that we do this challenging route. While I agreed it was important that my body adjust to the higher altitude, I did not think it was worth the effort and was concerned that the ordeal would leave me too weak to make it the top. The energy I expended getting to School Hut should have been conserved for the summit attempt. I regretted bartering away my strength for the sake of acclimatization. I searched for Betty and Tom below, but they were nowhere in sight. I wanted to warn them to turn back and hoped that they had enough sense to avoid our fate.

Kay and I closed the gap to School Hut. After three hours of hiking, including one after first sighting, we arrived. Nestled on a rock perch at 4,700 meters (15,400 feet) on Kibo Peak, School Hut was a ranger training facility with a few campsites. It was tantalizingly close to Kibo's volcanic rim. It beckoned like a siren and made me forget what I had already endured trekking this far. In spite of my ordeal, I was seduced by the alluring summit rising just above me. Delusion hoodwinked me into thinking that I could have made it to the top and back in short order.

My mind snapped me back to reality. If the route to School Hut had been this difficult, there was no way I would reach the top with what little strength I had left. I overestimated my ability and underestimated how difficult the climb would be. I regretted going on this frustrating hike and having to stop short of the summit. Remorse gripped me, and I vented by kicking the ground with my boot.

Kay and I slumped against a large boulder to recuperate for the downhill trek. We traded energy snacks. I begged her for some sugar bursts, and she gave me a few. Minja waited nearby, preferring as usual to stay aloof. He seemed by nature a quiet person but also trained as a guide that it was best to leave clients alone and provide assistance when needed.

"Congratulations, Kay, you beat Martina Navratilova," I said, giving my teammate a high-five.

"Woo hoo, I sure did! I'll have to tell my daughter."

I was happy for her. She did it. Kay climbed higher than a tennis champion. It was an incredible feat. As for me, I had to settle for outdueling Harry Street, a Hemingway character who didn't even exist. Thousands of climbers, men and women, old and young, even my wife, reached the summit. I wondered if, in the end, I would be among them. I wanted to send my wife a message and waved my phone in the air but could not catch a signal. I had to wait to text her again back at camp.

Kay and I chatted with a young German couple that stopped at School Hut to spend the night before their final ascent. I lamented that we had to go back to Camp Three when it made more sense to follow their lead. If we stayed here, we could acclimatize overnight at a very high altitude and put ourselves in a good position to reach the summit. Instead, we had to take a long trek down to Camp Three and then another full day's hike to Kibo Huts before ascending. It seemed like a lot of wasted time and energy.

The sun blazed down, warming my body and drenching me in sweat. I took a swig of flavored water to cool off and looked around. A rock wall rising high above camp sheltered it from the wind currents blowing off the mountain, calming the air. After our encounter with the sandstorm, I was glad that we were at School

Hut enjoying clear blue sky. Boulders and loose rock littered the mountainside, debris left over from age-old eruptions. The barren wasteland reminded me how close we were to touching the heavens, even though we were still bound to earth like ants on a giant mound. Kilimanjaro was so omnipresent that I felt small and insignificant.

The wind suddenly changed course and swept into camp ferociously. It battered the aluminum buildings with a clang that sounded like a passing train and almost blew away the German group's pitched tents. Kay and I hid behind the large rock where we were sitting, and Minja moved over to huddle with us. The brisk wind buffeted us from three sides and coated our clothing and lungs in dust. We could see, taste, touch and smell the earth. I choked and coughed.

The wind gusts died down after about ten minutes and clear skies reappeared. Kay and I laughed in disbelief at the freakish windstorm as we dusted ourselves off. I was glad we weren't hiking when it hit. Tom, Betty, and August were somewhere down below, caught in the middle of it.

We rested at School Hut for about twenty minutes more before hitting the trail again. The time was almost noon, and we wanted to return to Camp Three before sundown. August claimed that the entire hike would take four hours, but we had already trekked well over three and were not even half way. According to his plan, we still needed to stop at Kibo Huts and head down on a loop that I guessed would take at least three more hours. I assumed that the most difficult portion of the day's hike was over but was still apprehensive about the return trip. I coaxed my muscles to move again. Taking a rest break seemed to have done more harm than good and reminded me how sore my body felt after four days of hiking. There was something to be said about moving on and not letting the pain register in the brain.

We marched downhill at a moderate pace for almost an hour until we rejoined the main trail. Minja pointed uphill in the direction of Kibo Huts, while Kay and I insisted on heading downhill to Camp Three.

"No, Minja, we're not going that way. We're going back to camp," Kay said firmly. Minja did not say a word and continued to point toward Kibo Huts.

"No way, Minja," I said, pointing in the opposite direction. "I'm tired. We need to go back."

Minja started to take off toward Kibo Huts, as if he were expecting us to follow him.

"Minja! We're going down to camp," I said, raising my voice and using lively hands gestures to make it clear to him that we were not going to follow him no matter what August said. Rest and recuperation were my priorities, not acclimatization. "Look, Minja, don't worry. I will talk to August."

Minja gave in and skulked as we turned toward Camp Three. August was going to get an earful from me when I got back for sending us on this seemingly senseless hike.

We headed down in the early afternoon. Although the descent was less strenuous than the climb, loose scree left me slipping and sliding precariously on the trail. I wore gaiters to protect my legs from the onslaught of loose gravel and rock, but they did little to stop me from skating downhill. My hiking boots fared well heading uphill, but their thick rubber soles could not find a grip on this steep stretch of slope. I lost my balance a few times and did some comical pirouettes with my hiking poles to avoid falling unceremoniously on my buttocks. I cursed the ground when I fell on my side and slid over sharp rocks that scraped my flesh.

My mood deteriorated with the weather. Clouds laden with moisture grew thick and dimmed the landscape until the daytime looked darker than it should have. With the threat of rain looming, I wanted to hurry back to the campground as soon as possible, but the trail slowed me down. My hips and knees acted as shock absorbers and bore the brunt of my shifting weight whenever I slid. My emotions swung from disgruntled to worried when I started to feel pain in my joints. I hoped the soreness would go away after I had a chance to rest my legs. I wondered what Minja would have done if I tore a muscle or threw a hip out of joint on the trail because I didn't think that he would have been able to bring me back by himself if I were injured. I needed to make it to the campsite on my own. I certainly did not want to wait in the wilderness for hours while my guide went for help.

Kay and Minja hiked ahead but slowed down for me. I caught up with them not far from Camp Three. She noticed my limp and asked, "Hey, what happened? Are you all right?"

"No, I'm not. My legs are killing me," I told her through gritted teeth. "I keep sliding and falling on the trail. My knees are shot."

"Sorry about that. Take it easy. We're almost to camp."

"How about you? How are you doing?"

"I'm fine, but this whole day has been frustrating," Kay said. "It's ridiculous. This hike took a lot longer than four hours. It's been more than six hours for us, and who knows how long Tom and Betty will take."

I agreed. "This is much too hard to do right before trying for the summit. I'm going to have a talk with August when he gets back."

We made it to Camp Three in the late afternoon. Pain shot through my legs with every step. When I tripped over a rock, the shock reverberated through my knees so sharply that I thought I sprained a muscle. I picked up the stone and threw it away in anger. As I limped into our campsite, my arms and hiking poles flailing, I yelled at the first porter I saw, "Where's August? I need to talk to him!"

"On the mountain," he told me with a sheepish look on his face. I stormed off to my tent, casting my poles aside in disgust. I barricaded myself inside and fumed until my anger subsided and gave way to sleep. I stayed in my tent for hours to unwind and settle down enough to come out. I ignored the cook's calls for a snack. I dashed off a short message to my wife, the only one I knew who could cheer me up. *We made it to School Hut and back, but I'm in bad shape. Hiking today was a mistake. My knees are in pain. Hope to feel better tomorrow on hike to Kibo Huts. Miss you very much. Love, ME.*

I stared at the screen for a couple of minutes hoping for a response from Jing. Then it came. Her words soothed my soul. *I'm sorry to hear that, hon. I hope you feel better tomorrow. I'm praying for you. Miss you lots. Love you!*

Her words made me feel better. I reread the messages she sent me over the past few days and found them comforting. Even though she was far away, she seemed very close. Her words encouraged me like an angel of mercy. I looked at the daypack she gave me and found it comforting. It had been my constant companion on this journey.

Betty and Tom staggered into camp with August just before dark, more than eight hours after they left. The commotion of scrambling men who sprang to action when they returned caused a small ruckus outside. I tried to extricate myself from my tent to meet them but had to move slowly to avoid a relapse of pain in my legs. I massaged my legs with some heat rub and worked the joints until I could crawl out.

I stood up and gazed up at ever-present Kibo Peak rising above me. The clouds disappeared, and the mountain looked spectacular in the light of the setting sun. For a moment, I forgot about life's challenges, stresses, and calamities. After such an arduous day, I found the view mollifying.

I headed gingerly to the mess tent where the others gathered for dinner. I ducked inside and saw my companions' faces. Tom seemed tired and Betty exhausted. Kay looked fine. August was nowhere to be seen. I blurted out, "Are you okay? How are you holding up?"

"Tired," Betty and Tom said together.

"I imagine. Where's August? I need to talk to him about this. Today's hike was absolutely unacceptable," I said. As the one who organized the trip, I felt partly responsible for making sure that the climb went well for everyone.

"He's probably in the cooks' tent," Tom said. "I think we should wait until after dinner and talk to him together."

"Alright," I grumbled. The four of us agreed that the acclimatization hike was not worth the effort and that we needed to talk to August to let him know we weren't happy with the hike, the flooding, and other mistakes made on this trip. Tom suggested that we offer advice to help his team improve. I was grateful that he was a reasonable voice in this situation. If our guide had been around when I came back to camp furious, I would have yelled at him. Cooler heads prevailed.

We commiserated at dinner over the day's disastrous turn of events. Tom recounted their experience. They were caught in the miserable sandstorm Kay and I saw at School Hut, but they made it through and arrived at camp about an hour after we left. Hiking to Kibo Huts at August's insistence, Betty and Tom spent so much time resting there that they had to rush back to Camp Three and barely returned before dusk. Their journey took well over eight hours, twice as long as our guide's estimate.

After dinner Tom, Kay and I met August at the picnic table while Betty headed to bed. Unlike the previous night's deep freeze, the evening was warm enough to sit outside. The twinkle of stars and lights from camp stoves and flashlights illuminated the darkness. We turned off our headlamps and spoke in low voices to keep the conversation amongst ourselves. August sat next to us in his canvas safari hat, the light reflecting in his eyes as he waited for us to speak our minds. If he knew we were ready to give him an earful, he did not let on.

Tom began. "August, we appreciate what you and your team have done for us on this trip. We know you've worked hard and done a lot for us."

"Thank you," he answered.

Tom continued, "You're welcome. However, there are a few things we need to bring up with you."

"Okay."

"We all agree that today's hike was not a good idea," Tom said. "It wasn't easy. It was a lot longer and harder than we expected. Some of us aren't feeling well now, and we think it might have jeopardized our chances of reaching the summit. It would have been better for us to go on a shorter acclimatization hike today and then spent the afternoon resting."

"I understand," August said. He seemed to consider what Tom had to say. Hesitating for a moment, he finally said with measured words, "It is very important to acclimatize so that you won't get sick."

"Acclimatizing won't matter if we're injured or exhausted and need to be evacuated from the mountain. We have to be healthy enough to get to finish the climb," I interjected, keeping my temper in check.

Tom continued, "We're also concerned that there aren't enough guides with us who speak English. What if one of us gets into trouble or is injured? What if we have to be rescued from the mountain? We have no way to communicate with each other. You don't have any radios in case we're stranded."

"I see." August did not sound defensive and genuinely interested in hearing what Tom had to say. "I will see what I can do about the radios, but we do have a rescue plan."

We thanked our guide for his dedication and commended his team for working hard to help us reach the summit, singling out the cooks for doing a good job feeding us. We suggested some ways he could improve. I advised him to change the itinerary to include an overnight stop at School Hut. Tom suggested that he buy some two-way radios and send his guides to English classes. Kay told him that he should have hired more guides so that one climber didn't monopolize his time. Although August did not admit that the day's hike was a mistake, he agreed to consider our suggestions. We emphasized that heeding our advice would help his future clients enjoy a better trip.

After our meeting wrapped up, we bade each other good night and headed to our tents. I turned on my headlamp and picked my way through the campground, careful not to trip on loose rocks and trigger more pain. My legs and knees felt better than they did when I returned to camp but still stiff and vulnerable. The warm air soothed my skin, an improvement over the frigid temperatures we experienced the night before.

I thought about August. I appreciated his dedication but was dissatisfied with his performance. I considered him a diligent and caring man, but he inadvertently led our team into trouble. He seemed so concerned about altitude sickness that he did not consider whether hiking in such extreme conditions as we had to School Hut would leave us weakened and unprepared for the final summit push. It was certain the hike affected Betty, who looked worn out and was struggling to continue after the day's events. School Hut may have led to her undoing, and I didn't know if she would make it the rest of the way. Aborting the climb would be another setback for her after failing once to climb Kilimanjaro. Conserving her strength by dispensing with the acclimatization hike — or going an easier one — might have improved her chance of success.

As the trip progressed, Betty relied more and more on August. He stayed with her on the trail, carried her pack, and ran errands for her to keep her going. While he seemed to take it in stride, Betty's demands were unrelenting and put a strain on his ability to help the rest of us. Kay, Tom and I were relatively self-sufficient, although we would probably need more assistance on Kibo Peak. With four climbers and three guides, I wondered what August would do if a crisis befell the team en route to the summit.

Thanks to the acclimatization hike, I was no longer in the shape I needed to be in before the final ascent. For the first time, I felt worse at the end of the day than I did at the beginning. I used up much of my strength getting to School Hut, and the descent left me battered and bruised. My body could no longer keep up with my will, an odd sensation for someone who was used to thinking he was still young. At 40 years of age, I no longer had the vigor I had as a youth. I could regain my strength like Kay did when she became a marathon runner in her 50s, but I was in no shape to do that on Kilimanjaro. I was merely an overweight, middle-aged man who dreamed too big. I organized this climb on the crazy belief that it would kick start my life. Instead, it kicked my butt.

Hiking in the lowlands lulled me into the false belief that my allergies were in check, but the climb to School Hut dispelled that notion. After hiking through the swirling dust, I started to cough in fits again even after returning to Camp Three. I used the inhalers for the first time in days; something I loathed but had to do. I needed to take it easy and avoid pushing myself too hard or run the risk of illness right before my summit attempt. I wondered whether this setback ruined my chance of success. Altitude sickness I could handle. Not making it to the top because I burned myself out acclimatizing was unacceptable.

I slipped into the tent for the night too exhausted to clean up. I was more than ready for a good night's sleep. I barely made an effort to prepare for the next day's hike, throwing on a few extra layers of clothing and collapsing into my sleeping bag. The evening was still young, but I was too tired to write in my journal or comfort myself with music. The voices of the porters from nearby tents seemed distant and muted. I whispered a prayer and faded to unconsciousness, sleeping very well.

10. Calm Before the Ascent

December 31, 2010

I woke up with a start. It must have been early because no one called my name or shouted to let me know that it was time to get up. I sat up in my sleeping bag and saw the daylight filter into the tent through the thin fabric, warming my spirits. The thought crossed my mind through the haze of the morning grogginess that I was at the beginning of the end of our climb. Although we still had three days to reach the summit and to hike down to the Marangu Gate before it was over, this was the final leg of our journey.

The next two days promised to be even more difficult than our ascent to School Hut. We would spend the next day and a half trekking more than 25 kilometers (15.5 miles) and about 2,100 meters (6,900 feet) up and down Kibo Peak before stopping at a camp on the Marangu Route called Horombo Huts. We were scheduled to hike in the morning to Kibo Huts, the base camp below the Kilimanjaro summit, and then rest there until we headed to the top at midnight. The fact that we had to cross over one of the world's tallest mountains complicated matters.

I expected to be exhausted after the previous day's ordeal but instead was strangely refreshed from a good night's sleep. I felt reinvigorated with no signs of exhaustion or weakness. I moved my legs and bent my knees. They seemed remarkably limber and sturdy. It was as if the pain miraculously disappeared from my body. My prayers for healing seemed to pay off. I let out a cheer and thanked God for a swift recovery. Prayer gave me the strength to get through difficult times. I didn't know what lay in store for me on this trip, but I was reassured knowing that someone was looking out for me.

I wiggled out of my sleeping bag and pushed aside the tent flap. The morning was bright with clear skies. The temperature hovered at freezing but was still warm enough to walk around outside without a jacket. I was grateful that Camp Three sheltered us from the elements that lurked on Kilimanjaro.

Walking over to where the cook left our usual basin of boiled glacier water, I plopped down my carrying case on a large, flat lava rock and set up shop. Fed up with grimy hair that I hadn't washed since leaving Arusha, I ignored the crisp mountain air and washed my mop with shampoo. As I wicked the moisture away with my hand, the hair released steam and dried quickly under the intense sunlight. Tom walked by on his way to breakfast and asked with a curious look, "What, pray tell, are you doing?"

"I'm washing my hair! It's a nice day, so I thought I'd clean up a bit while I had the chance. I was starting to smell." I pretended to sniff my underarm.

"Well, I didn't smell anything!" he said with feigned seriousness. Betty and Kay saw me and smiled at the amusing sight.

My vain attempts to groom myself, like I did when I shaved on the second day of our climb, gave my companions plenty of amusement. While it's been said that it's better to look good than to feel good, I wanted to look *and* feel good.

Left cold by the washing, I headed to the picnic table for a warm breakfast. My palate resisted the usual regimen of toast, eggs, bananas, and other food items served day in and day out. To mix things up a bit, I asked the cook for some peanut butter he had stashed somewhere. After a few minutes of word play and hand gestures, he gave me the jar. The spread spiced up breakfast and made my morning. After almost a week of mountaineering, even basic condiments were simple pleasures.

We departed Camp Three for the last time. Kay, Tom and I left ahead of Betty, who labored to continue after five days of trekking. August stayed with her and carried her daypack. Minja guided us. We headed for Kibo Huts on the same trail that battered my knees during the acclimatization hike. I cheered when we passed by the detour to School Hut, glad to be done with it. Once again, a long line of porters passed us by with ease.

We stopped after an hour on the trail for snacks and boiled glacier water. I took a drink. The gritty silt did not taste too bad when masked by tropical fruit flavoring. I looked around and enjoyed the view. We stood in the middle of a large valley that looked as if it had been carved by an ice field that disappeared ages ago. I felt tiny in this wide open space that stretched from Kibo Peak to Mount Mawenzi, dwarfed by boulders deposited ages ago by lava flows. Amazed by the vast emptiness of the land around me, I exclaimed, "Wow, look at this place! We're in the middle of nowhere and far away from everything."

"Yeah, but isn't it beautiful? It's gorgeous here," Tom said. Kay nodded as she grooved to the sound of classic rock blaring in her ears.

"Hey, Kay, why don't you try pole dancing?" I joked, referring to a special dance that oxygen-deprived climbers perform with hiking poles at high altitudes when they're close to delirium. Tom gave me a curious look. Kay pulled the speaker buds out of her ears as I cajoled her. I said, "Here, try pole dancing. Like this!"

I grabbed my hiking poles, planted one on the ground, and held the other one up so that they looked like a long, vertical bar. I began to do a jig around them, clicking the heels of my leather boots. They laughed hysterically.

"Oh yeah, how about this?" Kay challenged me. Not to be outdone, she lifted her hiking poles above her head and gyrated her hips in a dance to the tune of some music I couldn't hear, doing a dance of her own. Tom looked amused. I egged him on. "C'mon Tom, you can do it too!"

"No, thanks!" He captured the moment with his camera. The reduced oxygen must have gone to our heads.

I hit the trail again happier than I had been in days. My body held up well, and my companions were a lot of fun. The levity lifted my spirits. We were heading for one of the heaviest challenges of our lives, so we might as well made light of it. Not only did I feel better, but I was mentally prepared for the final ascent. The route to Kibo Huts was steeper than I remembered when I slid down it the day before, but that didn't bother me. At least I wasn't heading to School Hut.

We stopped up trail near a cluster of big boulders that some climbers used as makeshift latrines. There were no bathrooms along the way, and those who couldn't wait until Kibo Huts went in the bushes behind rocks big enough to hide them. Those who forgot to bring toilet paper used whatever they could scrounge on the ground. I saw the revolting sight of soiled toilet paper scattered around the rocks. Who knew how long, if ever, it would take for the litter to decay at this altitude, where the temperature usually hovered near freezing. The cold air and perspiration left me too dehydrated to worry about making a pit stop on the trail.

I stopped to catch my breath and heard Tom announce that he found a cell phone signal. I pulled my phone from the daypack and sent a message to my wife. *Happy New Year, hon! Almost to Kibo Huts. Will try for the summit tonight. Sore but okay. Will text again as soon as I can. Wish I could be with you for New Years. Give our son a hug. Love, ME.*

I stared at the screen, half expecting a quick response from Jing, but the screen faded to black. She was with my son and her parents over a thousand miles away in Zambia at another wonder of the natural world, Victoria Falls. I reread her earlier messages. My wife's inspiring words encouraged me. They told me that she was as thrilled to receive updates about our progress as I was to get hers. I lost cellular coverage back on the trail, cutting my lifeline to the one I loved.

I rounded a bend and saw Kibo Huts in the distance on a small plateau at the bottom of Kibo Peak. The Marangu Route appeared like a ribbon on another ridge and headed our way. The distant trail was filled with clusters of climbers who trudged along the path, their legs dutifully marching in sync with their hiking poles, just as we were doing on the Rongai. Most were headed for a brief respite at the camp before heading to the summit. The tiny figures on the Marangu underscored how big and vast this mountain was — an appreciation that grew with every footfall.

The Marangu and Rongai routes converged just below Kibo Huts, and the merged trail grew considerably busier as climbers and porters jostled their way to camp. The camping spaces at Kibo Huts were first-come, first-served, upping the ante for groups to arrive earlier and claim the best spots. The trail widened to two lanes, allowing foot traffic to pass by in both directions with the faster trekkers passing the slower ones. The grade steepened as we made our final push to the camp. The ascent left me winded, but I didn't mind because it meant I was closer to the summit. I looked up at the steep face of Kibo Peak and saw the tiny speck I recognized as School Hut less than half way to the summit. It struck me that the final climb was going to be even higher and steeper than I thought. I gulped.

We arrived at the camp just before three p.m. after four hours on the trail. Kay, Tom, and I congratulated ourselves with high-fives and photos showing that we made it to Kibo Huts. At more than 4,700 meters (15,400 feet), the base camp was higher than many mountains. Making it this far was an accomplishment in and of itself, even though failing to reach the summit would have been a disappointment. I thought of Betty hiking behind us and wondered when she would arrive. She needed all the time she could get to tackle the final ascent, but at the pace she was going she would have less time than us.

We entered the campground and searched for our campsite. Kibo Huts were a patchwork of low-slung wooden buildings with sheet metal roofs and a sea of tents staked out in a clearing sheltered by a massive rock with the profile of a wizened man. The identical, brightly colored tents made from parachute-style fabric were arranged like a work of art. The climbers and workers milling around the huts were an eclectic bunch that ranged from sophisticated mountaineers dressed in the latest gear to underdressed porters walking around in worn-out jackets, tattered jeans, and loafers. The camp looked like a frontier outpost inhabited by transients who never stayed long but always left something

behind.

We found our campsite in a less-than-desirable location past the clearing that made the rest of camp look luxurious. It was perched precariously on the edge of the plateau exposed to the mountain face. One strong gust of wind from Kibo Peak would have blown our tents away. Climbers and workers who did not want to make the short jaunt to the latrines conveniently located near the huts turned the hillside below our campsite into an open-pit toilet. Toilet paper and feces littered the frozen ground below us. I breathed a sigh of relief that the cold kept the stink at bay. Unlike the giant boulders we passed earlier in the day, the hillside was wide open with little room for privacy. At this altitude, some did not care where they went. Nothing, not even bathroom etiquette, would stand in the way of their summit quest.

Kay, Tom and I bought cans of Coca-Cola from the camp office to celebrate our arrival. Kay and Tom wanted beers but were disappointed to learn that the camp ran out. We laughed that we might as well have been drinking in a freezer. I didn't care. I coddled my can of soda like an old friend. Sipping Coke on a frigid mountain was a fitting tribute to reaching the end of the so-called "Coca-Cola" Route. We took photos of each other posing with our beverages. After a week of gritty drinking water mixed with fruity flavor, enjoying a refreshingly cold carbonated beverage while freezing was just what I needed. The respite from carbonated beverages was good for someone like me who added a few pounds over the years indulging in sugary soda, but I thought it all right to have one after five straight days of hiking.

Kay cast aside her hiking boots and traded them for a pair of flip-flop sandals. Tom laughed. I joked, "Kay, you really need to relax. Chill out, will you?"

She grinned and said, "Oh, definitely! I just love my flip-flops.

There's no way I'm going to let the cold stop me from getting out of those boots."

"I'll drink to that!" Tom said. We raised our cans for a toast and let the dull thud of aluminum on aluminum honor the moment.

Cloud cover gathered and hid the sun. Cold air crept into my clothing and cooled my skin. I knew it was time to seek shelter when my nose started to turn red. I fled to my tent for warmth and a long nap.

The sound of voices near my tent woke me up from a deep sleep. The commotion sounded frantic, but in my grogginess I could not tell from the jumble of voices what happened. I sat up in my sleeping bag and was met by the dark gray of late afternoon. Opening the flap, I peered outside to look for the action unfolding nearby. A chilly breeze blew into the tent and displaced what little body heat was trapped inside. I heard August's voice but couldn't see him. He had returned, but I didn't hear Betty. I wondered whether she was with him. I put on some warm clothing and went to find them.

August stood near the mess tent talking to some porters. He looked animated, as if something had happened on the way. Betty was nowhere to be seen. I approached and asked, "August, what happened? Where's Betty?"

"She's in the tent," he reassured me, nodding toward the mess tent. I was relieved. "She's not feeling well and needs rest."

"Is she going to make to the summit, or will she be evacuated?" I asked, my voice belying my concern.

"I don't know. It's her decision. I asked her to sleep for now. She will leave two hours earlier than you at 10:00 p.m. so she can make it to the top by morning. We'll see how she feels when she wakes up."

I offered, "Then let her have my tent. It makes more sense for

Betty to have her own space if she's leaving earlier. I can share Kay's tent, and then we can rest until midnight. I'm sure she won't mind if I use hers. Let me ask."

"Okay," August agreed. I could not read his face in the dim light of the late afternoon. I hoped that he wouldn't press Betty to continue if she couldn't go on and that he had a plan to get her down the mountain if she needed to be evacuated. I didn't think he had the situation under control. If he was preoccupied with her, I wasn't sure whether he could help the rest of us on our summit attempt. I prayed that he'd manage. I walked over to Kay's tent, the sound of gravel crunching loudly under my boots, and spoke up, "Kay, are you sleeping?"

"No, not really," her muffled voice answered. She sounded exhausted. I hoped I hadn't pulled her out of a slumber. I said, "Betty made it to camp, but she's not doing well. August says that she has to leave earlier than us if she's going to reach the summit. It makes more sense for her to use my tent and us to pair up. Can I move into yours?"

"Oh, sure. Come on over," she said. I knew she wouldn't mind. Sharing quarters with Kay was a bit awkward, but under the circumstances, we didn't have a better alternative.

"Thanks." I went back to August and gave him the go ahead to move Betty to my tent. I asked him, "Can someone help me move my stuff?"

The porters moved my belongings, and August helped Betty. She slowly extricated herself from the mess tent. She stood up and slumped against August's shoulder. I asked her, "How are you doing?"

"I'm tired," she said, looking pale in the fading light. "Exhausted."

"Are you going to try for the summit?"

"I'll try." She limped to my tent, leaning on August, and disappeared. Evicted from the only home I'd known on the climb, I sought refuge in the mess tent before dinner. Much as I was disappointed for Betty, I was more nervous about my own summit attempt. Jitters shook my muscles; my mind raced to consider what I would face on the mountain. Waiting for the final ascent was like idling at the starting line before a marathon. Beset with anxiety, I worried about whether I had the stamina to scale Kibo Peak. It was a challenge on a scale grander than any I had ever known. At first glance, the face of Kibo looked doable under ideal conditions, but these weren't normal times. We had been hiking toward the heavens for days and still had a way to go.

Tired and sore, I wondered whether I was ready to tackle the summit in light of Betty's ordeal. The trek had sapped my strength and played with my health. My breathing was steady and my knees solid while I was sitting at base camp, but I would not know if what befell Betty would hit me when I faced Kibo. I too could succumb to altitude sickness. The feeling nagged at me that I would not have the endurance to reach the top. I dreaded the thought of suffering the same fate as Harry, watching helplessly as my dreams evaporated in the clouds. If I could not finish Kilimanjaro, I might not overcome other equally daunting obstacles. I might renege on leaving the Foreign Service and avoid taking a leap into the unknown field of writing. In the silence of the dimming mess tent, I resolved that I would never give up on the summit. My future depended on it.

Tom and Kay joined me for dinner. None of us said much; even Tom's usual humor was subdued. I could feel the pre-climb jitters permeate the tent. I picked at the spaghetti and gruel dispassionately and quickly retreated to my new home in Kay's tent. My belongings were piled in a corner. I set out my mattress pad and sleeping bag and laid down for one last rest.

Kay, Tom, and I were scheduled to begin our summit attempt at midnight. We had less than three hours to rest before our 11:00 p.m. wake-up call. Thoughts of whether I could ascend the final 1,200 vertical meters (5,600 feet) nagged at me, but I willed my body to relax and restless mind to still.

Minja woke me an hour before midnight. I marveled that I fell asleep and had a couple hours' rest. I wiped the rheum from my eyes. They felt tight from a lack of sleep, but I shook them loose. Kay sat in another corner gearing up. Working a kink out of my neck, I asked, "Did you sleep?"

"Not a wink," she said. "I just want to be over with this."

"I hear you." I wrapped several layers of clothing around my body to insulate it from the bitter cold. Two layers of woolen socks inside hiking boots. Two layers of long johns under hiking pants. Stocking cap. Heavy gloves. Balaclava, or ski mask, to cover the face. Headlamp attached to my forehead to light the way. Trusty hiking poles. At last I was ready to climb. As I waited for midnight to approach, I played with the crackers and tea that the cook set at the foot of our tent. I whispered a prayer and followed Kay into the freezing night air. The nighttime temperature plummeted.

I wondered if Betty had left for the summit as scheduled and went to ask August. The look on his face when I found him told me she didn't make it. "Where's Betty?"

"She's in the tent resting. We have to evacuate her."

"August!" Betty cried from inside my old tent. The guide scrambled to assist her. I wandered over to Kay and Tom, who were huddled together on the edge of camp awaiting their fate. I said, "Betty's not going to make it."

"Yeah, we heard," Tom responded. I could barely see him underneath the layers of clothing and the bright headlamp strapped to his forehead. "They're going to evacuate her at daybreak. I'm not sure they're prepared for this. They only have so many guides."

Between August, Minja, and the half-guide, half-porter Manda, the team was stretched thin. I thought aloud, "I hope all the guides are going with us. We're going to need all the help we can get."

"August said the park rangers will take her down the mountain. The guides should stay with us."

Too cold to stand around waiting, I went back to August, who seemed to be frantically giving orders to the porters. I assumed that some of them were going to help Betty evacuate and get her to a hospital. The look on August's face told me that things weren't going as planned. I asked, "Is everything all right?"

"Yes, don't worry." That did not sound reassuring.

"May I speak to Betty?"

"Yes."

I crouched next to her tent and said, "Hey Betty, it's Mike."

"Hi...hi, Mike," her voice quivered. "I can't go on. I'm not going to make it."

"I'm really sorry to hear that. Do you feel any better?"

"Not really. I feel awful. August told me they'll take me down as soon as they can. I should feel better when I get off this mountain. I have altitude sickness really bad. I'm nauseated and have a big headache."

"I hope you'll feel better soon. Take care of yourself, okay?" I said.

"Thank you, Mike. Thanks a lot for arranging the climb. I'll be rooting for all of you to reach the top."

"Thanks, Betty. Get some rest, and I'll call you when we get to the hotel, okay?"

"Okay, thanks."

"Goodbye."

I walked away with a heart weighed down by the altitude sickness and fatigue that cut short Betty's quest to climb Kilimanjaro. Twice she had failed to fulfill her dream to do what few Zambians achieved. I returned to Kay and Tom without a word. There was nothing more I wanted to say.

We waited half an hour in haunting silence before leaving camp. Wisps of snow and frozen breath threw shadows across my headlamp. The cold darkness punctuated by beams of light cast a surreal glow around me. I peered into the blackness and saw clouds of exhaled air and twinkling lights from nearby tents. I paced next to the sharp drop-off overlooking the makeshift toilet. I shifted my weight from foot to foot to generate heat while August's team made final preparations for our ascent and arranged to have Betty evacuated the next day. Half an hour seemed like an eternity.

11. The Face of Kibo

January 1, 2011

Kay, Tom, and I set off with August, Minja, and Manda for the summit just before midnight on New Year's Eve. Our headlamps lit a pathway amid the clutter of buildings, tents, and people. A glut of people caused a traffic jam as hundreds of mountaineers waited their turn to hit the trail. The long line snaked between buildings and rows of tents. We went to the end as more climbers fell in behind us, starting and stopping as we wound our way toward the Kibo trailhead.

The nearly 1,000-meter (3,200 feet) climb to Gilman's Point on the rim of Kibo Peak promised a fight. At 5,625 meters (18,450 feet), Gilman's Point was slightly lower in elevation than Kilimanjaro's highest point, Uhuru Peak, at 5,895 meters (19,341 feet). Although the ascent did not require special gear, climbers needed strength, endurance, and patience to scale the mountain in a crowd. If I survived the ascent, I still needed to hike another three kilometers along the rim of the volcanic caldron to the iconic wooden sign at the summit. I had 14 hours, from midnight until about two p.m., to reach the top and return to Kibo Huts before nightfall. Our group planned to do it by noon. That was our objective, but Betty proved that best-laid plans changed in thin air.

I felt as good as I could before I climbed. My breathing was steady, reinforced by a couple puffs on the inhalers to make sure my air passageways were clear. My legs and knees were sore but fit. I was mentally prepared for the ascent. I reassured myself that I could do it and dismissed the nagging concern lurking in my mind.

The cold nipped at my face as the line of climbers slowly wound its way to the trailhead. I peered into the darkness and looked at the night sky sprinkled with lights and stars. I knew what the mountainside looked like in daylight but was glad that I couldn't see it. August said that many mountaineers thought it better to climb in the dark. I did not mind being blind to the challenge in front of me because ignorance kept me going.

A litany of shouts and whistles rang in the New Year, startling me. I was so engrossed in the climb itself I had forgotten that I planned to celebrate New Year's on Kilimanjaro. The sounds echoed through the campground, amplified by the stillness of the night. Twinkling headlamps jiggled in the darkness like a fireworks show. While the impromptu celebration by other climbers was a far cry from the festive galas happening all over the world, it left a memorable impression. It signified to me not only the New Year but my personal rite of passage from diplomat to writer. I cheered silently as the past faded to history and the future took its place.

The traffic jam started to move up the slope, and the crowds thinned as more climbers hit the trail. We started to do the "Kili shuffle," waltzing our way together in a samba line, step by step, up the face of Kibo. The festive mood left me feeling upbeat. Like the little engine that wouldn't quit steaming up a mountain pass, I pressed on and thought, *You can do this. You can do it. Do it.* Our group jostled for position, passing some idle climbers and waiting behind others. The constant starting and stopping to wait for others made the climb more strenuous. It was coldly comforting to overtake slower-moving people, not so much because I was competing with them, but rather because it reminded me that I was still moving. Whenever someone went by me, I was reminded that I was only human. A group of elderly Asian mountaineers breezed past me as if they were on a leisurely stroll. Young or old, man or woman, fit or husky — nothing mattered on Kibo as much as a high tolerance for altitude and pain. I felt empathy for a handful of doubled-over climbers who were probably not going to make it to the top. A strong, fit-looking young man sat on a rock, apparently stricken with altitude sickness, gasping for air.

We stayed on the narrow gravel trail to avoid patches of scree loose enough to send us sliding downhill. August and Minja hiked in front while Manda fell to the rear to make sure we stayed on track. I marveled that they went up almost effortlessly sans headlamps with their daypacks and ours. August explained, "We don't need light. We know this mountain well." A veteran of hundreds of climbs who claimed he once did it solo in less than 11 hours, August amazed me. Despite my earlier complaints about his performance, I was glad that the talented mountaineer was my guide. I was going to need all the help I could get.

The trail steepened. It went uphill at a sharp incline for half an hour before it began to switchback across the mountain face. Our group hiked in the darkness with only headlamps to light the way. Stealing glances up and down the slope, I looked around to survey what little I could see. The night sky was awash in stars that stretched across the heavens but looked small against a wall of blackness. The camp was a small cluster of lights far below. A serpentine ribbon of light from climbers' headlamps followed the face from Kibo Huts to Gilman's Point high above. The line showed how far I needed to go. The longer I hiked, the farther it seemed to be, leaving me discouraged. I wondered whether my eyes played tricks on me or if I simply misjudged the distance.

I turned off the music pounding in my head to tune in to the sounds of the mountain, crunching gravel, and others' voices. My heavy jacket insulated my body from the cold and muffled the sound like a space suit. Despite hundreds of people nearby, I felt alone and isolated in a surreal place not unlike the moon — cold, dark, quiet, and oxygen deprived. Lonely.

We hiked an hour before taking a break. I took a swig of water but had no appetite for food. I felt fine until I stopped moving and everything fell apart. A wave of fatigue hit me. The air left my lungs, leaving me breathless. I felt sluggish. A crushing headache came on. My face grew hot and flushed in the dim light. My body succumbed to the intense climb. I tried to hide from the others the fact that I had just been hit with altitude sickness. I did not want to slow them down. When the group set off again, I drew on what remained of my strength and kept climbing.

The trail grew steeper at each switchback, making the ascent more difficult. I set my sights on reaching each bend to help motivate me to go on. The gravity of the climb finally hit me. Nothing I did could have prepared me mentally or physically for this. At full strength and at lower elevations I might have made it to Gilman's Point, but not after what I had been through. I was too exhausted to continue. The symptoms of altitude sickness hit me like an avalanche, and I could no longer hide it. My body screamed for rest. I asked Kay and Tom weakly, "Can we stop?"

"We just did," Kay answered. "Are you okay? You look really

tired."

"I'm not feeling so good. I need to rest. Sorry about this."

"No need to be sorry. Let's rest and get some energy into you. Your body's not getting enough nourishment," she said. I appreciated her thoughtfulness. Kay had a keen sense of sports nutrition. She tried to give me packet of energy gel. "Here, eat this."

"I can't. I'm feeling sick. I don't have the appetite."

"Mike, please eat it. You need some energy."

"Okay," I said. I didn't have the strength to argue. I ripped the packet open and oozed some gel into my mouth. It tasted awful. I felt like throwing up but forced myself to swallow it. We went on, but the energy boost had little effect.

Five minutes later, I needed to stop again. August came over to me and gave me a look that reminded me of the ones he gave Betty. With inquisitive eyes, he asked, "Can you continue? May I help you?"

"I'll be fine," I lied. I did not want the attention. I felt guilty keeping the group waiting high on the mountain not far from the summit. I said, "Okay, let's go."

My boots felt heavy, and I started to drag my feet and stumble on the trail. I felt woozy through the growing nausea and lightheadedness. My thoughts became less coherent except one nagging feeling — that I needed to stop climbing and go back down. Two minutes later, I stopped again. At long last, after 10,000 feet and five days of trekking, I ran out of steam 200 meters below the rim. I could see Gilman's Point just above me but couldn't will my body to move. I was spent.

Reality overwhelmed me and buried any justifications I had for doing the climb. I was a fool for thinking that I could challenge this mountain. I was too weak and small. I sorely overestimated my abilities and was paying for my arrogance. In the end, I was just a middle-aged man who wasn't built to climb mountains and was crazy for thinking that I could. Like Harry Street, I was a mortal with lofty ambitions whose dream had been crushed by the merciless Mount Kilimanjaro. Through the fog clouding my eyes, teetering on the verge of collapse, I thought I saw a twisted rock that looked like a frozen leopard. It reminded me of my fate.

"I...I need to...rest. You...you go on without me," I told my companions with a trembling voice. My legs were failing me, my breathing giving out, and my will conceding defeat. I was not going to make it to the summit on my own. I felt trapped on the mountain face, unable to go up or down. All I could do was rest. I slumped against a rock and tried to keep my eyes open.

Kay and Tom were worried about my condition and wanted to help, but there was little they could do for me. Kay tried to feed me more gel, but I waved her away.

I sat staring blankly at the darkness closing in on me. I started to keel over, but August caught me before I toppled over. I dimly heard him say through the fog, "Michael, can you hear me?"

"Yes," I said, my eyes closed and head spinning. I felt faint. I could feel nothing but August holding my arm and propping me up. The blackness started to close in.

"Can you go on?" I heard August ask me. I shook my head. "No, I don't think I can make it."

"Then let me help you," he said. Taking my hiking poles and slinging his arm around my shoulder, August helped guide me up the trail. I started to move and leaned on him to keep me steady. My head spun with dizziness and lightheadedness, but moving helped clear my head. I vaguely noticed Kay and Tom hiking ahead with Minja while Manda hovered nearby in case I needed assistance. At times, it seemed as if I were being carried until I realized each time I stumbled that I was still walking. August kept me from falling and made sure I stayed on the path.

Led by August, I picked my way along the trail. The terrain turned rockier and the bends more frequent, yet somehow I managed to keep my footing and continued hiking. I looked up and, through the dim light of the early morning, saw Gilman's Point within reach. The rock ledge at the edge of the volcanic rim inched toward me like a slow-motion dream. *You can do this,* an inner voice told me. *You can do it. Do it.*

I stumbled on a large rock and fell toward the earth, taking August with me. He jerked me back up and set me on my way again. As I gave him a hoarse thank you, my stomach lurched. It took all I could do not to vomit where hundreds of other climbers tread. Manda moved behind me to keep me from tumbling downhill. I stumbled several more times before reaching the last steep step below the rim. Gilman's Point was just a body's length above me. August and Manda helped guide me the last few feet.

I gave it everything I had to clear the ledge. Lobbing myself onto the rim, I landed unceremoniously on my knees and rolled out of the way of other climbers' boots. I stood up with wobbly knees and blinked away the blurriness. Through the haze I saw a gorgeous sunrise shimmer in the faint light and one of the most breath taking views I'd ever seen. Scattered mountain peaks and rippling clouds blanketed the horizon. The dark silhouette of Mount Mawenzi rose in front of me, reminding me how high we climbed. *This must be what heaven is like,* I thought. I was living Harry's dream on top of Kilimanjaro.

12. The Rooftop of Africa

January 1, 2011

It's been said that Kilimanjaro's height and the flatness of the surrounding plains offer some of the best views on Earth. I believed it. As I looked across the Serengeti toward distant lands, the first rays of the sun appeared on the horizon, casting radiant hues across the land. The light illuminated the steep face of Kibo Peak and the expansive alpine desert below us. My watch read eight a.m. Time seemed to slow with the sunrise.

I thought of Jing, far away but ever close to me. One year before, she was standing at this place on Gilman's Point. How I wished she could have been with me to share this moment. I wanted her to feel once again the exhilaration of being on top of the world.

I whispered quiet thanks for surviving the mountain face. I made my way over to a boulder away from the throngs of climbers milling around Gilman's Point and sat down to battle the effects of altitude sickness. I rubbed my blurry eyes and tried to knock them into focus. My body was weak and fatigued and my legs throbbed with pain. I massaged my muscles as deeply as I could through multiple layers of clothing to loosen them up. I tried to find my equilibrium to counteract the nausea and lightheadedness, but it was a difficult balancing act. I had no appetite but forced myself to eat some of the energy goo Kay gave me. I puffed on my inhalers but did not think they would do any good. My breathing seemed to be the only thing unaffected by the high altitude. It was going to take everything I had to make it to the top.

My ordeal was far from over. Gilman's Point was a false summit. The real one still lay a few hours ahead at the apex of

Uhuru Peak. My eyes followed the trail as it circled the rim of the Kibo crater to the summit several kilometers away. I sighed, dispirited. The 270-meter (900 foot) rise was not as steep as the ascent to Gilman's Point, and the path was in good condition and dry with a few patches of snow and ice. Still, the route looked intimidating. I had my work cut out for me.

Exhausted, I did not know if I would make it to the summit even with August's help. I was grateful that I could rely on him. I could not have gotten to Gilman's Point without him, and I knew he would assist me to the top of Kilimanjaro if I wanted him to, but I needed to make it on my own. I did not want to be carried to the summit by our guides. That would have been a hollow victory.

I was going to get there by myself. *You need to do this*, I told myself. My mind taunted me. *If you can't handle this challenge, there's no way you'll leave your job. You'll end up just like Harry and watch your dream die.* I was surprised by the harsh tone of the voice inside my head. My mind was caught between logic that told me to be cautious and a will that ordered me to keep going. A lot more was at stake than bragging rights or a photo opportunity. Kilimanjaro was testing me in a way that only the most difficult challenges in life could, like resigning from the diplomatic corps. The pressure to play it safe was immense. As a diplomat I was, in a way, at the Gilman's Point in my career. I could go ahead and resign, or I could turn back. My future would change dramatically once I quit, and doubts over whether I had made the right choice would nag at me. The voice in my head told me, *You need to do this. You need to follow your dream. Keep moving.*

A steady stream of climbers passed me by as I rested at Gilman's Point. Kay, Tom, and the guides waited more than twenty minutes until I gathered enough strength to continue. I was grateful that they stayed with me. Our group was primed to reach the summit, but I was holding them back. Delaying any longer might make them sick too. It was unhealthy for any of us to stay too long at this height. We had to reach the top and descend as quickly as possible.

I left Gilman's Point hobbling from the jolts of pain in my legs and knees as I navigated my way around clusters of boulders that littered the rim. The dizzy stupor brought on by altitude sickness dissipated, leaving me aware of my other ailments. I might not have been old, but I felt my age moving at an agonizingly slow pace. The pain came in waves as I moved, shocking me whenever I stumbled on a rock or shifted my weight to avoid a boulder or ice in my path. To take some of the pressure off my knees, I leaned on my hiking poles like a pair of crutches. They propelled me forward slowly. Minja shadowed me, but I insisted on hiking to the summit without his help.

On the way to Stella Point, I found a rhythm and shuffled a bit faster than molasses. Still, I urged Kay and Tom to go on ahead. After making sure I was doing all right, they picked up their pace and were soon out of sight. Other climbers passed me as if I was standing still, but I didn't mind. I would have rather progressed at a snail's pace than been carried off the mountain. At least I was moving on my own.

It helped that the hike along the volcanic rim was more gradual than the face of Kibo. The trail meandered past Stella Point to Uhuru Peak on the far side of the rim, cutting a path through jagged scarps that stood on one side like giant sentries and a slope on the other that tumbled into the Reutsch Crater. I peered into the volcano's caldera and shied away from the edge to avoid falling into the Ash Pit, a dune of ash at the bottom of the crater. Dingy brown rock and gravel worn from centuries of erosion dominated the terrain. The once-mighty glaciers covering Kibo Peak retreated long ago, leaving behind patches of snow and ice that remained in the shadows. I imagined that this forlorn alpine desert looked much like the surface of Antarctica absent its white blanket.

The mild weather softened the harsh surroundings and made the difficult climb more enjoyable. The sun cast an ethereal glow across the landscape, brightening the mountain's earthen palate, deepening the shadows, and painting the sky in shades of brilliant blue and frothy white. The stunning view lifted my spirits, and for a while I pressed on giving little thought to my ailments. Although the weather throughout our climb was as good as it could have been, I didn't expect conditions on the rooftop of Africa to be so nice. I could not have asked for a better day to summit. I was tempted to unzip my heavy jacket and take off an undershirt, but I kept them on to protect my pale skin from the intense sunlight. I had already been hit by so much adversity that I didn't want to add sunburn to my growing list of aches and pains.

After an hour of slow going, I arrived at Stella Point. As I crested the rim, I was greeted by a spectacular view of the Northern Icefield. Stunning glaciers graced the northern and southern flanks of the mountain, leaving me in awe at their majesty. Raked by the sun, beautiful and serene, the sheer walls of blue and white ice jutted into the sky like shining towers. In spite of their impressive size, I knew that I was seeing the final remnants of what were once massive glaciers that covered the entire peak in a colder age. Kilimanjaro now dwarfed them, its brown mass dominating the landscape as far as the eye could see. I was torn, lamenting how far the snow and ice had receded and yet glad that I did not have to confront them on the trail. I might not have been standing at Stella Point if I did.

I savored the view. The Serengeti spread out across the horizon as far as I could see under a blanket of low-lying clouds, punctured occasionally by the sharp reliefs of Mount Kenya and its mountain neighbors. Kilimanjaro's rotund profile rolled in ridges and hills down to the lowland plains. Covered in scree, its slope looked deceptively gentle. I realized how steep it was, however, when I watched climbers glissade down the slope in hiking boots. They cut through the loose rock like Alpine skiers as they sped downhill at astonishing speeds toward Barafu Huts on the Machame Route. I admired these seemingly fearless souls who braved the risk of injury or death for the thrill of using a more difficult route. I did not relish the prospect of perishing in a rockslide like three mountaineers did in 2006, or of falling ill to other ailments caused by a hard, fast ascent. In icy conditions, the way became even more treacherous, requiring climbers to cut ice steps or wear crampons. Our route might not have been quite so difficult, but it certainly wasn't easy, and I had the scars to prove it.

I left Stella Point feeling better after a short rest. I set off hobbling at my slow, methodical pace as Minja followed me. The trail to Uhuru Peak steepened, leaving me winded again. Altitude sickness bore down on me as it did on the way to Gilman's Point, and I rested more frequently. The distances between rest breaks grew closer and closer together. Struggling to move, I found myself starting and stopping at every oversized rock. Each one I passed was a minor victory.

I saw a bevy of climbers milling in the distance around the summit sign on Uhuru Peak. They disappeared and reappeared like apparitions amid the jagged rock formations standing in my way. The view was encouraging; the distance was not. I still had a long way to go. The summit remained aloof even after I exhausted my energy trying to close in on it. The mountain seemed to taunt me, throwing ever more obstacles at me and daring me to expend all my energy to reach it. I needed to get there soon, before the cutoff time forced me to turn around. I prayed that I would have the endurance to make it and get down before sundown.

I ordered myself to keep moving. Pain and fatigue gripped my body. I dug my hiking poles deeper into the gravel. My boots weighed me down and jarred my knees each time I lifted a foot. I zeroed in on the boulders and rocks in front of me and chose new targets to achieve, counting each footstep, as I passed them. One meter, two meters, three meters, four; I slowly closed the gap between Uhuru Peak and me. Altitude sickness numbed me, and the world slowed to a standstill around me save the blurred images of climbers who passed by on their way to the top. Hiking in slow motion, my senses slipped into a surreal world where nothing existed but the summit.

A chunk of lava lying on the trail blocked my way. I couldn't move around it and stopped, exhausted. I needed to rest. Leaning on my hiking poles, I buried my head in the crook of my arm and felt the world slip away. The jacket sleeve shrouded my eyes in darkness, my consciousness fading to black. I was dizzy and wanted to collapse. I sensed Minja next to me, ready to catch me if I fainted. *This is too much for someone like me to handle,* I thought. *I can't go on.*

Then I heard a voice that could only have been in my thoughts. *Don't stop. Keep going. You can do this. You need to do this. You are not alone.*

My head snapped to attention. I wondered if I was hallucinating, but it didn't matter. The encouraging words I heard were not an illusion. Casting the dizziness aside, I planted my hiking poles in the dirt and took off. I passed one more hill and hobbled to the bottom of the last slope leading to Uhuru Peak. Just 50 meters (165 feet) away, the summit opened up before me like the gates of heaven. I nearly fainted with relief as blood rushed to my head. The place that had been in my thoughts and dreams for so long was finally within reach. It beckoned for me to come. I drew on my remaining energy and waddled like a goose toward the golden spire of Kilimanjaro.

Kay and Tom saw me and waited at the top with big smiles. Behind them, I saw a stranger wave at me. A man dressed in a safari shirt and khaki shorts tipped his hat to me and smiled as if to say, *You made it. Well done.* The image dissolved and rose into the clouds above Mount Kilimanjaro. Harry. I had gone where he could only dream. I might not have died and gone to heaven like him, but it felt like it. After five strenuous days, four freezing nights, and an all-night hike, I was standing on the rooftop of Africa. I was so overwhelmed with emotion that I wanted to cry but was too tired to let the tears of joy flow.

Kay and Tom gave me hugs and high-fives. They cheered, "You did it! Congratulations! Feels great, huh?"

"Yes, it does! We...did...it. Congratulations!" I said, stammering for breath. The final push to the summit took a lot out of me. I gasped, "Amazing. Absolutely amazing."

13. What Comes Up Must Go Down

January 1, 2011

As I stood atop Africa's highest mountain, a thousand thoughts rushed through my mind. I had reached the summit. While some thought of it as a victory, I was more relieved that the mountain didn't beat me! I thought of Betty lying in a hospital in Arusha, recovering. Climbing Kilimanjaro wasn't so much a conquest as an uphill battle for survival. And a downhill one too. I survived the ascent but still had to get down. Wavering and listing like a battered athlete, I wondered if I could handle this new challenge. I certainly wasn't ready when the descent from School Hut thrashed my legs and knees.

Dozens of people milled around Uhuru Peak, admiring the view and waiting their turn to take photos with the iconic wooden sign. When it was ours, Kay and Tom pulled the guides and me in for a series of photos in front of the famous sign that read:

CONGRATULATIONS
YOU ARE NOW AT
UHURU PEAK TANZANIA 5895 M A.M.S.L.
AFRICA'S HIGHEST POINT
WORLD'S HIGHEST FREE STANDING MOUNTAIN

With a big grin, standing as tall as I could, I hoisted my homemade laminated placards. I thought of my wife, who stood where I did one year before, as I held the "I Did It" sign aloft. I suddenly realized that it should have read "We Did It" to honor her successful climb. I was happy that both of us shared this experience even though we did not do it together. I thought of my son and wished I could have given him a big hug. I raised the "Naysayer's Club" sign, smiled for the camera, and recalled those who had been critical of me. I resolved that from that moment on, whenever I felt intimidated by them, I would recall standing on the summit of Kilimanjaro and rise above their criticism.

After our photo session, I was too tired to stand and wandered over to a stump-size lava rock away from the crowds to rest. Kay, Tom and their guides already spent more than half an hour waiting for me, but they had to wait a while longer. I needed time to rest and gear up for the descent. Everyone else in our group seemed ready to head down but graciously let me be. I sat alone with my thoughts.

I looked out over the horizon toward the bluish-white glaciers of the Northern Icefield, the only snow and ice in sight. The view was fantastic. I could not believe how fortunate we were to have been blessed with balmy, almost spring-like weather. The sun was out, the air temperature mild enough for me to remove my heavy jacket and enjoy the sunlight in my sweatshirt.

I dallied on the summit for more than half an hour, longer than I should have. I was thrilled to be there and dreaded the long trek to Horombo Huts several hours beyond Kibo Huts. Kay reminded me that it wasn't healthy to remain at high altitudes too long, but I was loath to move again. I estimated that we had eight more hours and 20 kilometers to go, not to mention the descent down the face of Kibo, before the day was over. Although hiking downhill should have been easier than climbing, I could not get School Hut out of my mind. I hoped that my body would hold up on what threatened to be a grueling descent.

I departed Uhuru Peak with Kay, Tom, and the guides in the

early afternoon. We left later than August would have liked but still had plenty of time to get back before sundown. After my long rest, I felt better and tried to stay in front of the group so I wouldn't hold them up. Kay said, "Hey, you're doing great. Keep it up and you'll be down in no time."

"Thanks!" I said, saluting her with a hiking pole as I passed. The return to Gilman's Point was gradual enough to keep my frailties in check. I felt more like my old self until I slipped on a patch of ice in the shadow of Stella Point and nearly fell. I skated on the ice away from the crater's edge. It reminded me that my physical condition was still tenuous and that altitude sickness bedeviled my motor skills. I needed to take it easy. I wasn't off the mountain yet.

I returned to Gilman's Point much faster than it took me to reach the summit. At the ledge overlooking the face of Kibo Peak, I held on to the wooden railing and glanced over the edge. It was an incredibly long way down! Even after following the volcanic rim for hours with endless views of the horizon, I was still amazed by how high we climbed and the steepness of the mountain face. I appreciated all the more the tremendous effort Kay, Tom and I made scrambling to the summit. I could see why it was better to go at night.

The mountain face that we ascended in the dark seemed like a different world in the daytime. The afternoon sun cast a bright glow across the land and drew a contrast with the ridges and rock outcroppings so sharp that the scene looked as if it were painted by hand. Kibo Huts were mere dots in the valley several kilometers below. The face was so steep and riddled with scree, gravel and rock that it could have easily doubled as a Black Diamond ski run. All I needed was a pair of skis to fly down the hill. I stared down the slope, my heart pounding. I suddenly wished that I had learned some basic mountaineering techniques for traversing steep slopes. I had no way to self-arrest and dreaded to think what would happen if I lost control and slid downhill or crashed into a boulder.

Tom pulled up next to me as I looked over the edge and asked, "How are you feeling?"

"I'm doing okay," I said. "I feel much better than I did this morning, but we still have a long way to go."

I pointed at the horizon toward The Saddle, a high desert valley between Kibo Peak and Mount Mawenzi where we still needed to hike. Our destination, Horombo Huts, lay somewhere on the other side. Tom pointed down at the face of Kibo and asked, "That's true, but are you ready to go down *that*?"

"Um, sure," I said, not sure at all. "It's a long way down. How about you?"

"Sure, why not?" he said with his usual enthusiasm. "It looks fun."

"Fun? Are you kidding me?" I exclaimed and rolled my eyes.

"Not at all! It will be fun sliding down. Ready when you are!"

Paired with one guide each, Kay, Tom, and I jumped off the rim and hit the same trail we used to ascend. Tom and Minja went ahead, followed by Kay and Manda. I lagged behind with August, picking my way cautiously around a graveyard of boulders as I zigzagged downhill. I ground to a halt when Kay fell on the trail, slid downhill a body's length, and screamed at her guide, "Let go of me!"

"Kay, are you all right?" I yelled, making my way down to her. August and I slid over to her while Manda tried to help her to her feet. She yanked her arm away and warned him, "Get your hands off me!"

"What's wrong?" I asked. "Are you okay?"

"No! This guy is really rough with me. He doesn't 'handle with care.' I don't want him to touch me again. Can you take him?" Kay protested. August nodded and told Manda something in Swahili. Manda joined me while August lent his gentle hand to Kay. They headed downhill together without another word.

I was willing to put up with the junior guide's rough behavior but did not want him to pull me downhill. I realized why Kay reacted as she did when Manda took my arm. His hands were like a vice grip. He pulled me faster than I wanted to go, and several times I yanked back and warned him with gestures to take it easy. I communicated my displeasure by ripping my arm out of his hands and scolding him harshly with words and hand signs that I knew he understood. He seemed accustomed to diatribes from his clients.

Leaving the field of boulders, we entered a long, steep slope covered in scree and started to glissade. Tom and his guide barreled downhill so fast that they made it to the base of the peak in what must have been a land speed record. I wondered if they would lose control and take a spill, but they did it without falling. Kay and August were not far behind. Inertia, or perhaps Manda, grabbed hold of me and pulled me downhill at breakneck speed, and I slalomed, slid, and marched down the face of Kibo as fast as I could. I tried to glissade like a skier, but my poor legs flailed on the trail, slow to respond to my commands. If I were in better shape, I might have been able to pull off skating down the mountain, but I was in no condition to take any more serious hits that could put me in the hospital. I needed to put on the brakes.

The gravel and rocks that gave way under my boots softened the impact on my feet but left me with little traction. The fear of falling and my trusty hiking poles kept me erect halfway down the mountain face until I lost my balance and fell on my back. I triggered a small rockslide, and the scree swept me down the trail into a large rock that careened against my torso and bruised my side. My leg twisted as I tumbled. A sharp pain ripped through my knees and hips, and I gritted my teeth to avoid crying out in frustration. Scree rolled into my side. At least I stopped a rockslide, I thought wistfully.

I leaned on my hiking poles and slowly stood up. Manda offered me his hand, but I refused, knowing that his strong grip could rip my arm out of its socket. I growled at him for pulling me downhill so fast. He glared back and looked as if he wanted to yell at me in Swahili but held his tongue. I returned his stare with an angry look. I thought about telling him to leave but was stuck with him until I made it down the mountain face. As we started moving again, we lightened up. I lectured him a few times about not treating me like deadweight and working together as a team.

The shifting route wove back and forth across the face of Kibo Peak. The sun beat down and the cool breeze stilled as we descended. The rocks absorbed the heat, cooking the trail and leaving me sweating. The others were nowhere in sight. I wished that I was with them, resting up for the final hike to Horombo Huts, rather than fighting the inhospitable mountain, intense sun, and searing heat. Manda tried to coax me to take some shortcuts to save time, but I played it safe and stayed on the path. I wobbled, slid, and fell a few more times on the way down, each instance igniting throbbing pain that worsened with every step. My knees and joints felt like gelatin, making it difficult to move.

I sighed with relief when the slope leveled out but was disappointed to discover that the camp was still more than a kilometer away. It left me dispirited. Each victory seemed to end with yet another challenge. I turned to Gilman's Point for inspiration, staring up at the massive slope that I had just scaled. It had been years since I tackled a mountain, let alone one so high. Yet there I was, a middle-aged man feeling much older than my years, looking back at the huge challenge I had overcome. I felt better.

The trail passed through a maze of volcanic rock left behind millennia ago. Manda and I walked quietly through bizarre rock formations silhouetted by the afternoon sun. With our language barrier and the friction between us, we did not have much to say to each other, but I broke the silence and tried to make peace with him by shaking his hand and thanking him. "Asante sana. Thank you for helping me down."

Manda nodded but said nothing. He shook my hand. His eyes told me that he appreciated my gesture.

As I limped along, using my hiking poles to absorb the shock, I looked at the twisted lava rocks scattered on the ground. Picking one up, I noticed that it was shaped like a skull. The unforgiving environment on Kilimanjaro had turned volcanic debris into symbols of death. The mountain didn't cause my death, but like the rock in my hand, it twisted my body. I hoped that the contortions weren't permanent.

I arrived mid-afternoon at Kibo Huts. I thought about pleading with August to spend the night there rather than hiking another four hours to Horombo Huts, but he insisted that we press on to shorten our itinerary on the final day. Beyond Kibo Huts, we had more than 30 kilometers (19 miles) to hike before the climb was over, and heading to Horombo Huts would reduce the remaining distance by one-third. I reluctantly agreed. I burned up so much of my strength that I had little left to argue. I needed to recuperate, and fast, for yet another journey.

The cook announced that lunch was ready. I had not eaten a decent meal in more than 36 hours and hardly ate anything all day except energy goo, but I had no appetite and was too tired to eat. Sleep was a higher priority. I only had two hours until we departed camp, so I headed straight to my tent. If I was going to make it to Horombo Huts by nightfall, I needed as much rest as I could get. I ignored the cook's voice and fell to sleep as soon as I lay down on the sleeping bag.

14. The Saddle Sores

January 1, 2011

August woke me from a deep sleep. His baritone voice sounded distant as I vaguely heard him say that it was time to leave. My eyes tried to focus through the fog on my watch. The display read 4:30 p.m. Two hours' rest. I tried to sit up but fell back, weak and sore. I felt paralyzed by muscles stretched beyond their limits and screaming for relief. I struggled to bend joints that seemed to be frozen in place in spite of the warmth inside the tent. Frustrated, I shouted, "August, can you please come here?"

Moments later, his voice responded, "Yes?"

"I'm exhausted and can barely move. I really need some rest. Couldn't we stay here tonight?"

"I'm sorry, but we can't. Kay and Tom have already left. We must make it to Horombo Huts before nightfall. Don't worry, Mike, I will help you."

"Isn't there any way we can stay here?"

"No, I'm afraid not. We could always evacuate you from the mountain," August offered. His suggestion sounded sincere but came across like an ultimatum. After all I'd been through on Mount Kilimanjaro, I did not want to end the trip in a Tanzanian hospital. I answered, "No, I don't want to do that. I'll be out soon."

"I'll wait for you." Gravel crunched as August walked away. I looked around the tent. Kay's bags were sitting in a pile waiting for the porters to haul them to Horombo Huts. I didn't see Tom or her at the campsite before they left with Minja and Manda. I wished I were hiking with them to our next stop.

My numb hands forced my aching feet into a pair of tennis

shoes. After the long trek in hiking boots, I needed to wear something lighter and more comfortable regardless of the terrain. Surely the Marangu Route was easier than scaling Kibo Peak and manageable in casual footwear, I thought. I chewed my dinner, a granola bar, stuffed my belongings into my bags, and rolled out of the tent dressed in light clothing with daypack in hand. I declined August's offer to carry it for me.

We hiked slowly through a field of lava rock from Kibo Huts to the Marangu. August and I were virtually alone on the trail, passing nary a climber on the four-hour, nine-kilometer trek to Horombo Huts. I was able to avoid sliding and had better balance in tennis shoes, although I still used the hiking poles as a precaution. Walking was arduous. My muscles loosened up as I walked but continued to protest with every footfall. The hurt in my knees and joints refused to go away, although they held up under duress. As my muscles limbered up on the easy hike along the Marangu Route, the pain faded to a dull ache.

We hiked through The Saddle in the shadow of the magnificent, snow-capped Mount Mawenzi. I noticed two large rockslides that looked like a pair of Buddhas sitting cross-legged in prayer on the mountain face and wondered whether anyone else had seen them or if I was merely delusional. The effects of altitude sickness seemed to subside since my return to Kibo Huts, but I wasn't sure. The high altitude could have been playing tricks with my mind.

Mawenzi looked like a sundial as the sun dipped on the horizon above The Saddle, casting shadows on the high desert valley. It looked as if we had an hour of daylight left before sunset, not nearly enough time to make it to camp before nightfall. I hoped we wouldn't be caught on the trail at night because I had already had one bad experience in the dark. The terrain in The Saddle was flat and monotonous with little variation to lend it character, so my eyes searched for something interesting and focused on Mawenzi, one of the few reminders that we were still on Kilimanjaro.

August and I passed the time chatting at length about the climb. A quiet man, he let me do most of the talking. "Thanks for helping me make it to the summit. I really appreciate it. I couldn't have done it without you."

"You're welcome. I always try to do my best."

"I know," I said. "That's why I hired you. You were highly recommended by my wife's group that climbed last year."

August responded, "That's good. They were a good group. I like Jing."

"I like her too," I said, reminded of how much I missed my wife. "She inspired me to climb Kilimanjaro. I'm glad I had a chance to do the same climb she did. It's as if she's here with me right now. See, she gave me some of her equipment like my daypack and hiking poles."

I showed him my gear. August nodded as if trying to recall his memory of Jing. I thought it a good time to offer him some unsolicited advice. Not wanting to offend him, I broached the subject carefully. "I was sorry that Betty had to be evacuated. Thank you for getting her off the mountain. You and your team went beyond the call of duty to help her. So, thanks."

"You're welcome."

"I wonder, though, whether the hike to School Hut did her in."

"Maybe," he responded after some hesitation, his eyes staring at the trail. "We had to do the hike. Acclimatization is very important."

"I know, August, but you have to remember that not every climber is built the same way. Some of us need to rest longer before we hit the summit. The hike to School Hut wore us out. I think it might have led to Betty's evacuation and almost ended my climb. It wasn't just altitude sickness. We were exhausted too."

August said nothing. The sound of crunching gravel echoed in my ears. I continued, "Could you have planned our route so that we could have stayed at School Hut to acclimatize on the fourth day and then attempted the summit the next day instead of going down to Camp Three and back up to Kibo Huts? That would have bought us time to rest longer at Kibo Huts and spend the next two days trekking down. That seems more logical than the route we took. It's too late for us, but I think you should consider it for your next group."

"I'll see what I can do." August responded after a few moments. His face looked pensive. He seemed to take my suggestion in stride. An experienced guide, I knew that he could have dismissed me as a whining customer, but he seemed to understand that I had good intentions. We talked for a while about our families and lives back home and eventually fell into silence.

Two hours later, we were still hiking in The Saddle. Kibo Peak faded behind us, and Mount Mawenzi passed by my shoulder. I was struck by the desolation of this vast plateau nearly devoid of plant and animal life. As my eyes studied the route, I saw rocks littering the ground twisted into macabre faces like the skull I saw near Kibo Huts. I stopped to pick one up. It reminded me of tortured likenesses of climbers who writhed in horror at the prospect of failing to reach the summit. I thought it a cruel irony that this was where many climbers fell ill with altitude sickness and turned back.

I noticed piles of dusty elephant dung along the way and asked August how they ended up on the trail at 4,500 meters (15,000 feet). He said that elephants once roamed The Saddle but no longer after a fence was erected around Kilimanjaro National Park. Although I thought it unfortunate that the pachyderms had been deprived of their natural habitat, I was certainly glad that we didn't run into any en route.

At dusk, August and I left The Saddle and descended the mountain slope into a hilly area covered in vegetation. The trail became uneven and tricky to negotiate. The sun began to set, casting dark shadows over the land. I asked August how far we had to go and was met each time with the same response, "Not far." I was satisfied with his answer until the sun dipped low on the horizon, and as the light faded, began to worry about the distance and whether we could reach Horombo Huts before dark.

The grade steepened. The rocky trail passed over and around large rocks and erosion barriers. August switched on his flashlight to light our way, but the beam was not strong enough to keep the encroaching darkness at bay. The obscured, uneven path grew treacherous, and several times I almost tripped and fell. My hiking boots would have given me more traction than tennis shoes, I thought with chagrin. I stumbled and twisted my ankle, reawakening the intense pain in my legs. The ache that had nearly disappeared on The Saddle reappeared with a vengeance.

I vented my anger and scolded August for making us continue

so late in the day, although I knew it was my fault that we had gotten such a late start. The guide tried to help me and propped me up with his arm. It wasn't enough. As we stumbled down the dark trail into the blackness, I tried to walk but couldn't get any traction on the slippery rocks. August caught me as I wobbled. A rush of lightheadedness brought on by the lingering effects of altitude sickness hit me, and I felt the same sensation of being out of control that I experienced on Kibo. I could no longer keep steady, stumbling down the path like a drunk making my way through a dark alleyway.

Manda, who accompanied Kay and Tom to Horombo Huts, met us on the trail and grabbed my arm in a vice-like grip. August radioed ahead, and Minja met us minutes later. I tried to hike by my own power, but any strength I had left completely abandoned me, and I nearly collapsed. August caught me. Short of carrying me, the guides yanked, pushed, pulled, cajoled and hauled me to the campground like a malleable sack of flesh. My hiking poles and feet flailed uselessly on the trail as the three men dragged me downhill. Each time my legs bounced off a rock, the pain in my legs surged through my body, leaving me nauseated. Through the haze, I wondered whether my knees or legs were injured or broken. I was alive but fading into the same stupor I felt on Kibo Peak. My vision blurred, and I nearly passed out.

The guides dragging my exhausted shell of a body for almost an hour down the trail and hauled me into Horombo Huts late in the evening. I cried for joy when I saw lights twinkling in the darkness near the trail. The lights in camp helped bring me back from the trance I fell into on the way. My 18-hour ordeal up to and down the summit finally ended.

Manda and Minja left me at the tent, and I used my arms to pull my body inside. My legs were worthless. Kay, who had been waiting for me at the campground for hours, gave me a hug and congratulated me for making it back alive. I answered her with a weak smile and a sigh. As a reward for surviving, she gave me a can of warm Kilimanjaro beer, but I couldn't drink it. I couldn't consume anything. Once again, I passed up dinner. Instead, I simply crashed and drifted to sleep in my hiking clothes.

15. Routed on Marangu

January 2, 2011

I woke up at sunrise happy that this was the last day of the climb and that my journey was almost over. My mood was surprisingly upbeat given what happened the day before. I felt rested, but my body told me otherwise. A good night's sleep tricked my mind into thinking that all was well, but when I tried to turn over in the sleeping bag, my muscles burned. Nothing seemed to be broken, but my legs or knees were strained or worse. My only hope of getting off Mount Kilimanjaro under my own power was to outlast the soreness and go easy on my knees the rest of the way to Marangu Gate. I looked at the banged up hiking poles lying motionless in the corner. I hoped that my trusty friends could make it one more day.

I whispered thanks for surviving Kibo Peak and asked for the strength to get off the mountain without winding up in a hospital, praying that the pain wracking my body would cease. I had faith that I would finish the climb and make it home safely. My highest priority was getting down without ruining my knees.

I thought of my family and was anxious to see them again. I couldn't wait to tell my wife of my adventures. She knew firsthand what I went through. Life would return to normal after I went home, but it wouldn't be the same. I had changed. Kilimanjaro changed me. I planned to write my letter of resignation from the diplomatic corps and tender it when I returned. The battering I took on the mountain reminded me of the reality of Foreign Service life, where the stresses could be as challenging as climbing Kibo. As I prepared to leave the mountain behind and consign it to memory, I pledged to do the same with my job back home. Unlike Harry, I would recover from my wounds and change my life. At forty years old, I was finally ready to tackle it.

Kay awoke and began to rummage through her bags. It was my cue to clean up. Grabbing my toiletries and a change of clothing, I fought my way out of the tent, tripped on a canvas tarp in front of the door, and landed on my side against a large boulder. My battered right knee slammed into the ground as I fell with a thud. I cried out in agony and banged my fist in the mud to channel the pain and frustration. Little good it did! I was caked in mud.

"What happened?" Kay's voice asked.

"I had an accident!" I grunted, flinging slime off my hand and fuming. "Great, just what I needed! What else can go wrong?"

"Don't jinx yourself. You never know," Kay warned. She had a point. I scraped the dirt and mud from my clothing, scooped up the toiletries and clothing I had unceremoniously flung to the ground, and hobbled toward the bathroom. I waddled without my hiking poles, the first time I'd been without them in two days. My knees were stiff, but the pain was not as sharp as I expected. August saw me and walked over to ask again whether I wanted to be evacuated. He was obviously concerned about my condition after what happened on the way to Horombo Huts, but I refused. After all I'd been through, I wasn't about to end the climb being hauled down in a stretcher. The worst Kilimanjaro could throw at me seemed to have passed; I was sure I could handle whatever was yet to come.

I went into the bathroom, a faux chalet in the middle of rows of bunkhouses with identical Alpine styling. It was the first facility with running water and flushing toilets I'd seen in six days. I felt like a wanderer coming in from the wilderness, awed by the fact that the lavatory was clean with rolls of toilet paper. I washed the grime from my face and neck at a lone working sink and watched the residue swirl in the sink. The water ran cold, but I didn't mind. It felt great to wash away days' worth of grit. Just one more day to go until I returned to civilization and a hotel with a bed and shower.

I joined Kay and Tom the last time for breakfast in the mess tent that had become our nomadic sanctuary. It was the first time we had a chance to sit down together and commune since the final ascent.

"How are you feeling?" Tom asked.

"I feel awful, but thanks for asking," I said sarcastically.

"Well, what did you expect?" he smiled. "You came back pretty late last night. Were you partying up on the mountain?"

"No way, buddy," I said. "I got back from Kibo Huts and took off long after you left. August's team almost had to carry me here. What time did you pull in last night?"

Kay said, "Oh, about 6:30 p.m., a couple hours before you. We were worried you weren't going to make it. Glad you did."

"Yeah, me too," I said. I turned to Tom and asked, "So, Indiana Jones, what was it like going down Kibo? I couldn't believe how fast you were going. You must've made it down in twenty minutes. It looked like you were skiing! What you did was crazy."

"It was incredibly scary!" he grinned. "The guide wanted to do it, so I just held on. What a rush."

"You were amazing," I told them. "Kay, you breezed up and down this mountain, and Tom, you just plugged away. I was doing fine until I ran out of steam on Gilman's."

"Hey, it happens. We're just glad you're all right," Tom said. He clapped me on the shoulder. Kay said, "Don't speak too soon. We still have to get off this mountain. I can't wait for a hot shower."

"Don't worry! I can't smell a thing," I joked, tapping on my nose. "I guess you won't be meeting Thor on this trip."

She laughed, "Yeah, I guess not. Maybe next time — if there is a next time."

We chatted over breakfast about how fulfilling the climb was for each of us in spite of the challenges we faced. Betty's evacuation. Kay's tent flooding two nights in a row. Tom's tough hike to School Hut and back. My sudden bout of altitude sickness and bad knees. We reminisced about our adventures on Mount Kilimanjaro. We developed a strong bond with one another over the past week that would endure beyond the climb. We were no longer colleagues but friends who shared an unforgettable experience. Our mood was sanguine but tempered by the reality that our journey, for better or for worse, was almost over.

Tom, Kay and I divvied up tips for August's team that worked hard to support our climb. We paid each guide, porter, and cook a tip according to their job and services they had provided. August received the biggest tip, followed by his deputies, porters, and cooks. The cooks got a nice tip for serving the best meals they could with limited ingredients, as did Minja for doubling as a porter and guide. Manda's brusque demeanor earned him the minimum. Tom stuffed the cash tips in envelopes, crawled out of the mess tent, and gathered August's group together for a short ceremony to thank them for their help. Tom emceed and called every team member forward for a handshake, "asante sana" thank you, and a tip.

We set off at mid-morning on our final day of hiking. I guessed that it would take about five hours to cover the 21 kilometers (13 miles) to Marangu Gate. Kay and I went ahead with Minja and kept up a steady pace. Tom and August fell behind. Kay and I chatted along the way, a welcome break from three days of music that no longer inspired me. The aches and pains in my body were still evident, but I felt better than expected on the trail. Like I did on the summit, I wanted to avoid holding up the group by lagging behind.

I took in exotic views of the landscape gracing the southern slopes of Kilimanjaro. Lush with unusual plants and trees, the scenery was a welcome respite from the desolate high desert and the alpine landscape of the Rongai Route. The fertile highlands along the Marangu Route were filled with windswept views of stunted forests and swaths of vegetation unique to the mountains of East Africa. The first trees I encountered after Horombo Huts were the dendrosenecios, bizarre cactus-like groundsel trees with trunks like palms and topped with spiky leaf rosettes. A cactus-like flowering plant known as the lobelia deckenii dotted fields of

bunchgrass. Unlike humans, this vegetation was hearty enough to handle the harsh climate.

My legs held up well on the descent except for the occasional ache when I kicked a rock or stepped down an embankment. Kay's rapid, bouncing pace kept us moving at a steady clip even while I tried not to overexert myself. For a few hours, I hiked in a nice groove that I hoped would stay with me all the way to the gate.

Signs of altitude sickness disappeared as we descended. The air lightened and the pressure lifted like a weight from my chest. My appetite returned when we stopped for a break, and I consumed large quantities of snacks to satiate my starved body. My stricken knees remained weak, unaffected by the altitude.

The trail wandered through bunchgrass fields and strands of trees along the broad, gradually descending slope of Kilimanjaro with occasional drops into small ravines carved by glacier-fed streams. As we entered a forest in the subtropical lowlands, we were met by wispy bunches of old man's beard hanging from the trees like tattered voiles ready to spring back to life when the rains returned. The tree moss transformed the forest into a fantasy land and took me away from my infirmities.

The last campground before Marangu Gate, Mandara Huts, eluded us for hours. Kay and I joked that we had somewhere between five minutes and five days more to hike. Two hours later, the camp appeared like a mirage, a small organic settlement nestled in the thick lowland forest. We tromped into the encampment with Alpine-style chalets and pristine bathrooms and plopped down on a bench-size log. We shared a celebratory drink while we waited for August and Tom to catch up. Kay cracked open a can of Kilimanjaro beer and guzzled it down in a few gulps; I sipped a soda. I wanted a beer but thought it wiser to avoid drinking alcohol until the hike was over. We waited for August and Tom until our beverages ran dry and Minja announced that lunch was ready. My mind complained that it was a waste of time stopping for lunch so close to the end of our trek, but I scolded myself for being impatient and told myself to relax. It would take a while for the 'old' me to stop and enjoy life.

Kay and I sat down for lunch inside the dining hall at a massive table hewn from a large tree. I thought it progress to eat indoors instead of in a mess tent. Tom and August arrived not long after we started eating. Together we toasted our success with mugs of Milo cocoa that Tom prepared one more time. It had been days since I chuckled at the sight of him mixing drinks like a mad scientist. He took his drink very seriously. We ate our final meal of fried eggs, bananas, toast, and instant coffee. The cook must have given up trying to prepare original dishes and served whatever leftovers remained from our trip. The meal did not sit well with my stomach. I glanced at another table and salivated over the food they were eating, nearly going over to barter my eggs in exchange for some of their lunch.

After a short rest at Mandara Huts, we set off for Marangu Gate in the early afternoon. August said that the hike would take about three hours over steeper terrain than we covered from Horombo Huts, but I didn't mind. I could do it. The thick forest plunged the trail into shadow, letting in just enough sunlight to make clear that it was a gorgeous day. The land smelled earthy, with moist soil and heavy foliage all around. The woods were quiet with few signs of life save our group. We hiked alone in muted anticipation that the end was near.

We stopped at a mountain stream cascading downhill. Minja went to the water's edge and dipped his canteen in the stream. He offered me some. I wondered whether it was safe to drink but threw caution to the wind. It was glacier water, I thought, and besides, I'd survived much worse on Kilimanjaro. I took a sip. It was delicious. Its refreshing taste reinvigorated me and satisfied my thirst better than any bottled water I'd tasted. If it carried any impurities, I did not want to know.

The grade steepened with occasional drop-offs held in place by tree roots and rocks. The pressure of stepping down the sharp drops jolted my knees. I pulled my hiking poles from the daypack and wielded them like extensions of my arms to cushion the impact of my footfalls. They helped me keep up a brisk pace on the trail for more than two hours. I stayed ahead of the group to set the pace. As I descended drop-off after drop-off, the pain spread to my hips and torso. I responded by slowing down and taking measured strides, stopping at each step to lower myself down gently.

This strategy worked for another hour but ultimately failed when the searing pain in my legs intensified. My knees and joints burned so fiercely that I thought that they might need reconstructive surgery after the climb was over. Each step stung. Every movement felt as if my muscles and joints had been ripped to shreds. My legs begged for rest, but their cries fell on deaf ears. I was determined to end this once and for all — even if it meant that I ended up in a hospital. It came down to perseverance. I would not let my body stop me from finishing this challenge.

I hobbled along the trail for what seemed like an eternity until I reached the place where I was convinced the exit should have been. Instead, I confronted a sign informing me that Marangu Gate still lay three kilometers ahead. The news hit me hard. My temper flared, and I ranted against everything that I thought worked against me on the climb. The mountain. My body. The team that supported me. The park management. I fumed over my idiocy for being crazy enough to go on this adventure and risk everything for a dream. I shook my fist at the mountain and screamed, "Ahh!"

Kilimanjaro did not want to let me go. I escaped its clutches many times before, but this time it tried to break my spirit by throwing one more obstacle in my path. I was near the end. I would show this mountain that it could not conquer me! My eyes narrowed and my teeth clenched as I shouted that I would not let it take me down. I would defeat this monster if it killed me.

In my delirium, I started to gallop down the trail toward the gate like a mindless animal. I was determined to finish this once and for all. My hiking poles propelled me faster than I should have gone, even though I went no faster than a slow jog. I gave up keeping track of the others hiking somewhere behind me; I dared not look back in case I tripped on a rock or a root and crashed. My body could not keep up with my rage for long, and I floundered like someone in a losing battle. I was spent. I stumbled, fell to the ground, and collapsed on the dirt trail in a heap.

August was suddenly by my side. The guide who rescued me on the face of Kibo and patiently brought me down to Horombo Huts once again stood ready to help. He looked at me with mercy in his eyes. They told me that he was sorry that I was in pain and would help me to the very end. He asked, "Is anything broken?"

I felt my lower body. My swollen knees and joints burned. Pain sent shockwaves through my nerves. I rubbed my hands across my legs to make sure they were still intact. My bones felt bruised but not broken.

"I don't think so," I said weakly. He held out his hand and pulled me up. He offered to help me, but I refused. I was going to make it on my own power.

The others caught up and stayed with me to the end. My tantrum subsided, and I limped glumly down the trail, resolved to deal sanely with whatever remaining obstacle blocked my path. We crossed over a mountain steam and down a moderate slope at a slow creep.

Suddenly, the trees parted, and I stumbled into a clearing with a cluster of buildings. Marangu Gate! I made it! The view was so surreal that I could hardly believe my eyes. I thought it ironic that I had come full circle to where my journey began. Seven days, 90 kilometers (55 miles), and a mountain later, I ended up in the same place where I started. But I wasn't the same person who was here the week before. I had changed.

Hobbled as I was, I was in no mood to loiter at the gate but had to wait for August to sign us out of the park. I waddled into the gift shop and bought some souvenirs for my family. I purchased a blue T-shirt with a map of Mount Kilimanjaro for my son. I would be reminded of the climb whenever he wore it around the house. I bought my wife a safari hat with the mountain's famous relief emblazoned on the front to commemorate both our climbs. I opted not to buy the "I Climbed Kilimanjaro" T-shirt for myself because I already had a few mementos to remember my adventure — the aching pain in my knees and joints that would eventually fade but could, from time to time, flare up and remind me of the climb.

The last 50 meters from the gift shop to the van were the toughest of all. My muscles started to freeze up as I waited for August to finish, so I started off. Leaning on my faithful hiking poles, I set off down the path toward the parking lot, doing my best rendition of the "Kili shuffle." One step, stop. Two step, stop. Another step or two and another stop to rest my knees. Step, step, stop. A wooden carving of a leopard watched me curiously from across the campground.

After a long struggle, I reached a flight of steps down to the parking lot where the van waited to take us back to Arusha. The team watched me as I lowered myself down the stairs with my poles as if waiting to see whether I would fall. One step, two step, stop. A few more steps, then stop. I made it on my own power without toppling over. Beers cracked open like fireworks to celebrate the end of our climb.

We gathered for a group photo to remember the moment before driving away.

16. Moving On

January 2, 2011

The day wound down as we drove back to Arusha. I was relieved that I did not have to hike in the dark again. My legs got some much-needed rest in the van as I watched the subtropical forests pass by in a blur. As Mount Kilimanjaro disappeared from view, I thought about the climb. None of us had much to say after we left Marangu Gate bound for civilization.

A ring on my phone broke the silence. Startled, I fished it out of my daypack and answered, "Hello?"

"Hi, hon, it's me. Did you make it?" a lovely voice asked. It was such a relief to hear my wife's voice for the first time in a week! She knew my itinerary so well that she timed her call to coincide with my departure from the park. Surprised, I exclaimed, "Hi, hon! You called just in time. I made it to the top, but I'm pretty beat up."

"You made it? That's great! Congratulations! I'm proud of you."

"Thanks," I said. My voice shook from fatigue and the

van as it bounced over potholes and speed bumps.

"How was the climb?"

"It was good for a while, but I had a tough time on the summit. I was hit by altitude sickness below Gilman's Point and almost didn't make it. I made it back all right, but my knees are in bad shape."

"You poor thing," Jing cooed. "Come home and have a rest."

"I will," I told her as static interfered with the connection. "I'm losing signal. Please give my son a hug, and I'll see you at the airport tomorrow."

"Okay. I love you. Congratulations!"

"Thanks, hon. I love you, too."

The phone lost signal, and the call dropped. Hearing my wife's voice made me feel much better after another grueling day. I was grateful to have my cell phone. Without it, we would have had to wait to talk to each other. When she climbed Kilimanjaro without hers, I learned she made it back safely to Arusha after she used our credit card to withdraw cash.

Tom talked to his wife and told her the good news. Kay decided to wait until we reached the luxurious Mount Meru Hotel to call her daughter. August contacted the hospital in Arusha where Betty had been admitted and learned that she had been released and was now resting at the hotel. Her doctor cleared her to rejoin us for the flight home. After what happened to her on the mountain, it was good to hear that she recovered well.

We arrived at the hotel in the evening. The scene was comical as we trundled out of the van in front of the five-star hotel filthy and in desperate need of a shower. I'm sure employees were used to bedraggled climbers showing up to stay there after a week on Kilimanjaro. I tried not to drag dirt on my clothes and bags through the immaculate lobby.

After August arranged to pick us up the following morning for our departure, Kay, Tom and I checked in, and the van sped away. I collected my bag of clean clothes and accessories I left with the hotel before heading to the mountain and looked forward to swapping my dirty gear for them. We agreed to meet for dinner and parted company. I headed to my room, doing my best not to touch anything.

I made myself at home in the pristine room, scattering the contents of my bags on all available surfaces and sorting my belongings into dirty piles. I soaked in the shower, letting the hot water wash the grit from my body. I shaved the stubble from my face and put on a fresh set of clothes. Ah, relief! Stubborn remnants of the climb, from blisters and bruises to dirt under my fingernails, remained. I limped around the room and straightened up my gear for the trip home while a television program droned on in the background. My muscles felt stretched. A dull pain settled in my joints. It was going to take a while for the aching to stop.

I called Betty to see how she was doing. She sounded happy to hear from me and congratulated me on a successful climb. I told her how glad I was that she was doing better. I invited her to join us for dinner, but she declined and told me that she needed to rest. Wishing her well, I mentioned that we planned to rendezvous in the lobby the following morning for our trip home.

I met Kay and Tom at the hotel restaurant for a scrumptious African and western buffet. I piled on the food as if I hadn't eaten in a week and avoided any dishes that reminded me of the climb. I gorged myself on anything my eyes fancied.

We sat on the balcony overlooking the hotel garden. The moonlight cast a soft glow over the grounds as the twinkle of light from lampposts flickered like fireflies. Kilimanjaro faded to memory as we soaked up the casual ambiance that reminded me of an evening at an African safari lodge, sans the belching hippos. Tom said, "This is really nice, huh?"

"It sure is a nice change from eating in a tent," Kay said.

"Definitely," I said.

"Well, then, I propose a toast to our victory," Tom offered, raising his glass. "To victory!"

Our wine glasses clinked with a sweet sound that commemorated our successful climb.

"I think we should get awards for what we did," I said. "I was thinking about our accomplishments. Kay, I'm giving you the 'power award' for all that energy you had on the mountain. I couldn't believe how well you handled the climb. Not even Martina Navratilova can say that. It definitely helps being a marathoner."

"Thanks, Mike." I thought I saw Kay blush, but it was hard to tell in the dim light.

"Tom," I said, "You get the 'stamina award' for maintaining a steady pace during the entire trip. You were like the turtle that won the race. I was the rabbit that ran out of gas."

He laughed. "I never fancied myself a turtle, but thanks."

"Betty gets the 'courage award' for taking on the mountain twice and being evacuated both times. That takes a lot of guts."

Tom said, "Then you get the 'perseverance award' for doing the climb even though you were sick and injured, not to mention for staying out of the hospital. What you did was very inspiring."

I grinned. "Thanks, Tom. That means a lot to me."

A full week together climbing a mountain did not dampen our budding friendship. I enjoyed their company. After all we went through together on Kilimanjaro without arguments or friction, I hoped they would accompany me on another adventure. I asked, "Are you two up for a hike in the Himalayas? I really want to do the Annapurnas Circuit in Nepal. Care to join me?"

Kay and Tom looked at each other and then at me, surprised.

Quiet for a moment, Tom answered, "Sounds fun, but I'll have to get back to you."

"I'll think about it," Kay said. "Let me recover from Kili first!"

"Of course," I laughed. "I definitely need to recover. Think about it and let me know."

After dinner, I hobbled to my room. Sitting for more than an hour made my legs stiff again. I did not know whether they would fully recover or how long it would take. I needed to visit the medical clinic for a full checkup after I got home.

I sunk into the warm bed and let it draw me in. It felt so good after a week's worth of sleeping on the cold ground. My body was tired, but my mind was still awake with a flood of thoughts and emotions. I survived Mount Kilimanjaro. I remembered standing on the rooftop of Africa looking at the most amazing view I'd ever seen. It was as if I glimpsed heaven. I saw the earth from above — a world filled with beauty and promise yet filled with storm clouds. I was thankful for the opportunity to experience such a profound, life-changing moment and live to tell about it. The mountain better prepared me to live among storm clouds.

Another test lay ahead of me. I still had the daunting task of leaving the Foreign Service and embarking on a new calling as a writer. Resigning from the diplomatic corps promised more obstacles. After I submitted my letter of resignation, I would have to wind down my job as a "lame duck" among colleagues determined to climb the career ladder. Until I left, I would be waiting to move on while they passed me on their way to the pinnacles of their careers. The nefarious bureaucracy of the State Department that at times seemed to take on a life of its own, like the Kraken, was going to do its best to seize me in its tentacles and not let me go. I did not know how much damage it would do to me as I battled to extricate myself from it.

The world of writing was a big unknown. After years of lending my pen to the Department, I knew that I could write and was ready to put it to what I thought was a better use. I did not know if anyone wanted to read my writing or how to connect with those who did, but I was going to find out. It was a brave new world that I needed to explore.

I prayed that as I returned to real life, the challenges would not be as great as they were on Kilimanjaro. I hoped that the experience equipped me with the resolve and endurance I needed to rebuild my life and move past a midlife crisis that had me in its grip. Battered and feeling aged, I had not escaped the mountain unscathed, but like a hardened warrior, I came away with the mental toughness that I needed to fight inertia and the tendency to take the easy way out.

Drowsiness came over me, and I could no longer keep my eyes open. I fell into a deep sleep and dreamt of an epic struggle on an unknown battlefield.

17. Farewell to Kilimanjaro

January 3, 2011

I awoke early on my final day in Tanzania eager to catch my morning flight home to Lusaka, Zambia. My upper body felt refreshed after a good night's sleep; my lower body was more relaxed but still in pain. I would have to wait to talk to the nurse when I got home about whether I needed medical treatment. I couldn't wait to tell her that her efforts to help me recover from my respiratory illness worked. My body may have felt weak, but I felt younger and in better shape than I did before I left Zambia.

My spirits brightened when I thought about my wife and son. In just a few short hours, I would meet them at the airport in Lusaka for big hugs and kisses, like a soldier coming home. My in-laws would be there to greet me too. I missed them all. My loneliness might have been more acute had it not been for the connection I shared with Jing during my climb. Her uplifting messages were a godsend that kept me going. While I lost touch with her near the summit, I read and reread her messages whenever I needed an encouraging word. Soon, I would be back in her arms and hear soothing words from her instead of my phone.

I stuffed my belongings into my duffel bag, travel bag, and daypack. I somehow managed to fit the huge pile of dirty clothing that seemed to have grown larger overnight into my luggage, close and lock it. Dragging the overstuffed bags to the lobby, I joined the group. Tom chatted with August as Kay checked out at the front desk. Betty smiled when she saw me. I limped over and gave her a hug. She looked great — much better than the last time I saw her. I asked, "How are you, Betty?"

"Good! I'm much better now."

"That's great! Glad to hear it," I said. "What happened after you were evacuated from camp?"

"Well, the porters put me in a stretcher with wheels — it looked like a wheel barrow — and hauled me down to Mandara Huts. There was a really nice physician on her way up the Marangu Route who gave me some medical attention until a rescue team came to escort me. She was great."

"A Good Samaritan helped you? That's great!" I said. "Then what happened?"

"The rescue team took me down to Marangu Gate. They put me in one of August's vans and took me to the hospital. I ended up paying a lot of money for tips and the hospital stay."

"That's too bad," I said. Whatever Betty paid for her rescue was on top of the thousands of dollars she spent to climb. The park entrance fee covered her evacuation, but she had to pay the rest out of pocket.

"At least I feel better now."

"I'm so glad. I told Tom and Kay that you deserved an award for having the courage to try climbing Kilimanjaro twice. That's inspiring."

"Thank you, Michael."

After I finished checking out of the hotel, I turned around and saw Betty, Kay, and Tom chatting with August next to a mountain of bags. Once again, they were waiting for me.

We piled into the van with our gear and set off for the airport. None of us spoke much during our last hours in Tanzania. I stared out the window and watched the countryside pass by. Shops painted in exotic colors topped with rusting sheet metal roofs lined the road amid stands of palms so tall that they bowed and formed a canopy. Locals on bicycles or foot with children on their backs or goods on their heads crowded the shoulder. Vendors sat next to the highway selling a mosaic of fruits and vegetables. The subtropical forest gave way to semiarid steppes as we approached the airport.

I searched for one last look at Mount Kilimanjaro but could not see it behind the moisture-laden clouds that stretched across the grassy plain dotted with acacia trees. I knew it was there, somewhere, lying in wait like a leopard on the Serengeti. I pictured it as Harry Street did before he ascended to heaven — an unforgettable view of Africa.

18. Parting Thoughts

One Year Later

My adventure continued after I returned home. My family greeted me at the Lusaka airport with hugs, kisses, and warm smiles. My son was so excited to have me home that he made me a big "welcome home daddy" poster and hung it on the front door of our house. I hosted a reunion dinner with Betty, Kay, and Tom a few weeks later to share memories of our climb. Tom made my evening by fixing me a gourmet cup of Milo cocoa. I missed it so.

I spent the next few months after the climb resting and recuperating. Any lingering effects of altitude sickness vanished after I touched down in Zambia, although my allergies returned with a vengeance. My favorite nurse brought me back to health in short order. I hobbled and limped for a while, but my legs eventually recovered from the beating they took. Resting them was the best medicine. In time, I felt stronger than I did before the climb.

In late January 2011, I submitted my letter of resignation from the State Department. Many colleagues were surprised by my revelation but commended me for pursuing my dream to write. The Department sent me a standard form letter signed by a deputy stating that it regretted my choice but understood that I made it after careful consideration. If only it knew how much effort went into my decision.

I officially resigned in August 2011, and then plunged headlong into writing. I left the diplomatic corps with no regrets and felt free to pursue my new calling. I no longer felt like Harry from *The Snows of Kilimanjaro*, sacrificing my potential for the sake of an unfulfilling job that left me preoccupied with my own mortality, beset by predators and scavengers in a veritable death-in-life. I exorcised my demons. I held to my principles and stayed true to myself, no longer worried about changing my personality to suit the Department.

I was glad at midlife that God was with me every step of the way, from the final push to Uhuru Peak to the anxious moments when I told the Department goodbye. I needed all the help I could get. Relying on a power greater than myself gave me the strength and resolve I needed to overcome huge obstacles in my quest to find fulfillment. While some would say that I don't need a god to get through life, I'm glad I do.

I can't say that I've reached my ultimate destination, but life has been, without a doubt, more fulfilling for me since I climbed Kilimanjaro. More peaks and valleys are bound to come my way, but going over that hill better prepared me to tackle whatever may come my way. It taught me to go further than I thought I could.

On my final day in Zambia in July 2011, before moving to my new home in Thailand, Kay and Tom threw me a small farewell party. Kay gave me some energy goo as a gift, and I surprised them with plans to write a book about our adventure. They took it in stride and told me that they didn't mind being portrayed in this book and that they would consider trekking the Annapurnas Circuit in the Himalayas of Nepal with me. Someday, perhaps.

If you reached the top of Kilimanjaro, congratulations. You achieved something truly remarkable. I hope that my story rekindled memories of your own trip. If you tried to climb it but didn't succeed, take heart. Many never reach the top. Kilimanjaro park officials estimated that roughly 30 percent of climbers get to Gilman's Point, and many who make it that far turn back before the summit. You're well on your way to success. If you're thinking of trying again, you should weigh the physical, emotional, and financial costs and make any adjustments needed to get to the top. If you're in poor health, think twice. Any existing health conditions will likely worsen at higher altitudes.

Thousands of climbers stand on top of Mount Kilimanjaro each year. The number who summit annually is subject to debate, but I estimated that 38,323 people climbed it in 2010 based on the certificates my wife and I received for our successful climbs. Jing's certificate was number 79,816, while mine, issued one year later, was number 118,139. By my own estimate, more than 35,000 people climb the mountain every year with few fatalities. You can too.

The climb is not technically difficult and does not require special gear such as oxygen, and you don't have to be a professional mountaineer to reach the summit. That said, Kilimanjaro is not easy. Far from it. It is one of the toughest mountains accessible to novice climbers. Tens of thousands who try for the summit never make it. Kilimanjaro lore is riddled with stories of people who failed. The mountain has had its fair share of accidents and tragedies, such as a rockslide in 2006 that killed three people and left several others severely injured. More difficult routes such as the Western Breach lend themselves to more risk. Although the routes I hiked, the Rongai and Marangu, are considered "easier," they are still difficult.

Don't underestimate the mountain no matter how "easy" someone says it is.

Mount Kilimanjaro changed my life. The most challenging obstacle I've ever faced, it pulled me out of a midlife crisis and set me on the path to a better future. I hope that I never have to face a challenge like it again, but if I do, I'll be ready.

19. Learning the Easy Way

Here are some suggestions and tips for you to consider if you're preparing to climb Mount Kilimanjaro. In some cases, these are lessons I learned the hard way that I want to pass on to you. Some suggestions may not be applicable. Use your judgment and consult your guide if you have questions about preparing for your own climb.

1. Be in shape. You do not have to be in prime physical shape to reach the summit, but it helps. You should be in relatively good health before climbing Kilimanjaro. Get as fit as you can before you go because it increases your chance of success. If you are considering a climb, plan ahead and seek guidance from professionals on training for it.

2. Train. Preparing to climb Mount Kilimanjaro takes months of training. Do not underestimate the difficulty or the level of preparedness needed to succeed. If possible, do activities such as hiking that build endurance and improve your cardio-vascular system every day for extended periods of time. Aerobic and endurance exercises are more helpful than power exercises.

3. Acclimatization. Altitude sickness can get the best of any climber. Abide by the popular Swahili saying "pole pole" ("slowly, slowly"). Take your time while trekking; don't be in a rush. Allow your body time to adjust to higher altitudes. You will be hard pressed to reach the summit if you do not acclimatize properly. There's no magic pill to help you acclimatize — it just takes time.

4. Good respiration. A well-developed respiratory system may be the best indicator of whether you will reach the summit. If you are a smoker or have asthma, climbing may adversely affect you. Experts recommend that you stop smoking at least six months prior to attempting a climb. If you are asthmatic, have breathing issues, or are ill with a respiratory condition such as pneumonia, you may experience breathing difficulties at higher altitudes. Women are discouraged from climbing during pregnancy because of potential risks to the child.

5. Leg strength. It helps to have a strong lower body, good knees and hips because you will exert a tremendous pressure on them as you trek. This is especially true on the descent. If you have bad knees or joints, you may experience elevated levels of pain like I did.

6. Climb with friends. Go with a group of people you like. Avoid the tendency to cobble together a team based only on a mutual interest in climbing Kilimanjaro. If you do, get to know one another beforehand. You will spend a week together in a harsh environment that inevitably brings out the worst in people. Any conflicts you have with your teammates may play out on the mountain when you are in close quarters for an extended period of time. If you find someone annoying at sea level, they will surely drive you to distraction in thin air.

7. Buy quality gear. Don't buy cheap clothing or equipment. Purchase waterproof or water-resistant clothing made from breathable, synthetic fabric. Comfortable boots are your best asset. Climbers who wear ill-fitting footwear often come back with blisters on their feet or lost toenails caused by repeated smacking against the inside of the boot — an unsightly but survivable side effect. Preventing lost toenails is as simple as cutting them before climbing.

8. Moderate alcohol consumption. Some claim that higher altitudes intensify the effects of drinking alcohol, although research studies haven't verified this claim. However, drinking at higher altitudes can impair your judgment, leave you dehydrated and make you feel sick. It's better not to mix the two and stay sober when you're hiking. A celebratory beer at camp after a long day's hike should be fine.

9. Hire the right guide. Your guide is critical to your success. They can make or break your climb. Hire a professional. Don't cut costs by going with an amateur. Some Kilimanjaro guides have more experience than others. Don't go with an outfitter simply because they are the cheapest; likewise, there are many great guides and tour companies available to hire at affordable prices. Balance quality with cost. Avoid choosing one that charges you thousands of dollars more than you need to spend because in the end, climbing Mount Kilimanjaro is a great equalizer. No matter how much you spend, your support team cannot guarantee that you will reach the summit or have a rewarding experience.

10. Have a backup plan. There's a chance you may not be able to finish your climb. Decide what you'll do if you have to abort or cancel your trip. Our guide agreed to let us pay him after we finished the climb rather than charging us an upfront deposit. Few outfitters allow this. We thought this was a better option in case someone had to cancel.

11. Do your homework. Talk to someone you know who's already climbed Kilimanjaro for tips on preparing for your own. Thousands of people have climbed it; you may know some of them. They can give you advice on how to prepare. Read a guidebook or visit websites with in-depth information about the mountain. I listed some useful resources in the next chapter to help you with your research. Learn from others who know — don't end up discovering at 16,000 feet that you forgot something important.

12. Be inspired. Focus on something that inspires you to climb. Maybe it's your faith, family, or friends. Maybe it's a goal you've set for yourself. Perhaps you've caught the climbing bug and are starting your quest to conquer the Seven Summits, the highest peak on each of the seven continents. Think about what drives you to climb Africa's highest mountain because at some point you're probably going to question why you decided to do it in the first place.

13. Be safe. While Kilimanjaro National Park is generally safe, Arusha and Moshi can be dangerous. Tourists and climbers have been targeted by thieves, in some cases with weapons involved. Take extra precautions when walking around town. Do not carry valuables or be conspicuous. Consult your guide before leaving your hotel.

14. Protect your valuables. Before you fly, lock your bags with Transportation Security Administration-compliant locks. Non-TSA locks can be cut and thrown away during security inspections. Secure your entire luggage, including carry-ons. For extra protection, consider shrink wrapping your check-in baggage. They're less likely to be plundered in transit. When you're climbing, remember that your belongings will pass through many hands. Keep your valuables, especially money and travel documents, with you at all times, preferably in a neck pouch. Lock your bags on the mountain as an added precaution. While petty theft is rare on Kilimanjaro, it can happen.

15. Arrange lodging. Work with your guide to arrange lodging for the inbound and outbound portions of your trip before you head to Tanzania. You may want to stay in a basic lodge or hostel the night before the climb and at a more luxurious hotel after you finish. Arusha seems to be a preferred destination, although in some cases Moshi may be better if you're hiking the Machame, Marangu, Umbwe, or Rongai Routes. Moshi is grittier and, some say, more dangerous than Arusha, but it is closer to both Kilimanjaro

International Airport and the park and has a few decent hotels. Climbers usually spend one night in Arusha on the inbound and outbound portions of their trip. Some guides reportedly earn commissions if their clients stay at certain lodges. If you have the option to book your own lodging, you may find better deals doing it yourself.

16. Bring your Visa credit card. As of December 2010, Kilimanjaro National Park only accepted Visa credit cards as means of payment for the park entrance fee (US$742 in 2010). Cash, traveler's cheques, and other credit cards were not accepted. Although this is subject to change, you're better off bringing your Visa card if you want to avoid being turned away when you try to pay your fee.

17. Get some cash. I exchanged some U.S. dollars for Tanzanian schillings at a currency exchange when I arrived in Arusha. Years of traveling taught me to rely, if possible, on local currency rather than credit or debit cards, ATMs, or traveler's cheques for trips like Kilimanjaro when you don't need much local currency. Carrying some cash helped me avoid awkward moments when I could not find an ATM to access my bank accounts or cash a traveler's cheque. The international transaction fees can be high, so judge how much currency you need to exchange before completing the transaction. If you plan to use a credit or debit card, be sure to notify your financial institution of your trip in advance so your account is not flagged for a suspicious transaction and locked down.

18. Keep a contact list. Carry a list of local contacts, including your guide and hotels, so that you can call them if needed. The more information, the better. Write down the contact numbers for your country's embassy in Tanzania and the Tanzanian police in the event of an emergency.

19. Diamox or not. Diamox is an over-the-counter drug used to counter the effects of altitude sickness. It can be effective but may lead to temporary, not-so-pleasant side effects, including loss of appetite, numbness and tingling in the fingers and toes, a bad taste in the mouth, and blurred vision. Some climbers swear by it while others refuse to take it. I decided not to take Diamox. I don't know whether it would have kept me from falling ill with altitude sickness, but it might have helped.

20. Using the latrines. While there are toilets on the Marangu Route, the other routes have latrines with "squat pots." Get used to using them unless you want to head to the bushes. To use one, straddle the pot, lean forward, and hold on to something to steady yourself. Hold your pants away from the line of fire, plug your nose, and give it a try. Bring copious amounts of toilet paper, but throw it into the trash bin unless it's an open-pit toilet or you'll clog the plumbing. Good luck.

21. Sleep in your own tent. Your guide will provide tents. Unless you're with your partner for life, it's better to pay more for your own domicile. It gives you more privacy on the climb and helps you avoid those awkward moments when you're changing clothes in your tent or snoring.

22. Spot your tent. Note where the team pitched your tent. If you're close to the support team's quarters, it may get noisy at night. Make sure yours is not pitched in a swell where rainwater runs off when it rains. Ask to have your tent moved if it's not in a good location. As we learned on our climb, the porters don't always set up tents in the best locations.

23. Wear sunscreen. Put on plenty of sunscreen when you're climbing to avoid sunburn. At higher altitudes, the atmosphere is thinner and allows in more ultraviolet rays than at sea level. The sunlight can be intense, and your skin can burn easily. Use high ultraviolent sunscreen (70-power or above) frequently to protect your skin, particularly when you sweat. Even water-resistant sunscreen wears off when you sweat.

24. Take care of your muscles. Your muscles will inevitably get sore on the climb. Alleviate the sore muscles, strains, and aches and pain as needed with topical ointments such as Ben-Gay or Tiger Balm or a pain reliever such as ibuprofen.

25. Rest when you can. Get as much rest as often as you can when you're not hiking. Unplanned acclimatization hikes aren't necessary because your guide should have built them into your schedule. Extra hiking won't make much of a difference.

26. Use your judgment. Question your guide's advice if something seems amiss. Guides tend to apply a one-size-fits-all formula that may not be optimal for you. For example, acclimatizing may be good for those prone to altitude sickness, but it may not be so good for someone with no such symptoms who might be better off resting their weary bones. Your guide is your leader, but don't follow blindly. Have a dialogue with them if something does not sit well with you.

27. Emergency/evacuation plan. Talk to your guide, preferably before you start your climb, about their contingency plan in the event of an emergency or evacuation. Ask them how they will handle the remaining climbers when members of the group need to be evacuated. Ask how they will handle an emergency situation on the trail where no help is readily available. Make sure the guide has adequate coverage for all climbers and anticipates problems that may occur. Confirm that they have a first aid kit in the event of an injury and two-way radios for all guides. If you're not satisfied with their answers, hold them accountable for coming up with satisfactory solutions.

28. Cell phone. Buying or renting a local cell phone may not be necessary because your guide should make all the arrangements for your climb. Save your money. A cell phone is helpful to keep in touch with family and to make unplanned calls. If yours has international coverage, check beforehand to see if any local carriers have partnered with your service provider. As of December 2010, carriers with reception on or around Kilimanjaro included Safaricom, Vodacom, and Tigo. Coverage is spotty on the mountain. You are more likely to catch a signal from nearby towns and cities. You may consider purchasing a local cell phone if you're planning to stay in Tanzania for a while.

29. Entertain yourself. Between hikes you'll have downtime. To pass the time when you're not sleeping, have portable items handy that will entertain you when you're alone such as paperback books or electronic devices that don't need a quick recharge. Bring a deck of playing cards to play card games with other climbers during frequent downtimes. Playing cards are portable and a nice diversion from climbing and shivering in your tent. Make sure you keep them in a waterproof bag in case it rains. I brought my iPod music player and Kindle e-reader, and they came in very handy.

30. Meet your team. Get to know the guides, porters, and cooks who will help you fulfill your dream. Tanzanians are generally friendly and helpful. They go to lengths to help those they care about, including their clients. Learning a few phrases in Swahili, the local language, will go a long way to building rapport with your team. They will remember you as the foreigner who spoke their language. See Chapter 23 for a list of practical words and phrases in Swahili.

31. Pay decent tips. Many members of the support team earn very little on a climb. The pay is small but more lucrative than most jobs on the local economy since the guides and porters earn additional money from tips. They work hard for you. Giving them a decent tip is the right thing to do. There's no set rule for the amount, but a generous tip is reportedly 15 percent of the fee you paid your guide shared among all members of the team. Guides receive the biggest tips, followed by deputies, porters, and cooks. Place each tip in a separate envelope and give it directly to the worker to avoid tensions over how the money is distributed.

32. Donate extra gear. You may not need some of your clothing and equipment after you finish your climb. Many climbers donate extra gear to the team. It's a personal decision whether to give away your belongings, but your team will appreciate it. You can make a donation of used gear in good condition to any of the many porter support groups that help workers. Many are online.

33. Pack it in and pack it out. Don't litter. Properly dispose of all waste materials, including toilet paper. Some trash does not decay at high altitudes and will remain intact for decades, if not longer. Conscientious climbers pack it out and dispose of litter to preserve the environment and keep the park clean.

34. Mind the gap. Distances, times, and even names on Mount Kilimanjaro are imprecise. You may hear varying answers about your destination, how far it is, and how long it will take to get there. There are frequent discrepancies between the estimated times it takes to get someplace. Always take estimates with a grain of salt and understand that the answer often depends on whom you ask. Even landmarks aren't quite correct.

35. Spend time in Tanzania. Tanzania is a great place to unwind before or after climbing Kilimanjaro, and many climbers start or end their treks with visits to some of its popular tourist destinations, including the Ngorongoro Conservation, Zanzibar, and Dar Es Salaam. Ngorongoro offers great safari opportunities, while Zanzibar, an archipelago in the Indian Ocean about 50 kilometers off the coast of the mainland, offers a rich mix of African and Middle Eastern influences. Some flights from Arusha to Dar Es

Salaam stop in Zanzibar. Tanzania's largest city and its commercial center, Dar is a good stopover on the way to or from Kilimanjaro. Bagamoyo, the former capital of German East Africa from 1885 to 1890, is a historic town with some beautiful resorts on the Indian Ocean.

36. Transit issues. Climbers flying to Kilimanjaro International Airport near Arusha usually connect at Julius Nyerere International Airport in Dar Es Salaam or Jomo Kenyatta International Airport in Nairobi, Kenya. You will pass through Immigration and Customs at whichever airport you arrive in Tanzania. Flights from Dar to Arusha usually depart from the domestic side of Nyerere Airport, which you can access through the main entrance. Some opt to fly into Kenya and ride overland by car or bus to Arusha, crossing the Tanzanian border. Precision Air, a small domestic carrier, is the main airline flying into Arusha with a fleet of small, propeller-driven airplanes.

37. Passport and visas. Bring your passport with you. Tanzania requires visas for foreign nationals from many countries. As of this writing, visas could be obtained for a fee at Tanzania Embassies or High Commissions accredited to your country or upon entry into Tanzania. Check the Tanzanian Ministry of Foreign Affairs and International Co-operation web site at http://www.foreign.go.tz/ for the latest information on documents required to enter the country.

38. Immunizations. Research which immunizations, if any, you need and get them before you leave. Be sure to carry your World Health Organization Immunization Card, better known as the "yellow shot card," showing which inoculations you've had. Africa has a wide range of diseases ranging from malaria to yellow fever, so be prepared to get the shots you need.

20. The Who's and What's of Kilimanjaro

A.M.S.L.: Above mean sea level.

Acclimatization: A process of adjusting to a gradual change in environment, including altitude, allowing one to maintain performance as environmental conditions change.

Acute mountain sickness (AMS): An illness caused by excessive exposure to low oxygen pressure at altitudes above 2,400 meters (8,000 feet). If left untreated, AMS can progress to life-threatening high altitude pulmonary edema (HAPE) or high altitude cerebral edema (HACE). There are no specific symptoms other than reported resemblances to the flu, carbon monoxide poisoning, or a hangover.

Afromontane: A region in Eastern and Western Africa straddling the Equator where clusters of freestanding mountains or plateaus are surrounded by lowlands. Also known as sky islands, the mountains are stratovolcanoes with biologically diverse climate zones.

Arrow Glacier Huts: A camp at the base of Kibo Peak used by climbers who ascend Kilimanjaro via the Western Breach. The camp was destroyed by rockslides but is still used by many climbers.

Arusha: The largest city in the Kilimanjaro region and the primary jumping off point for Mount Kilimanjaro climbs and safari expeditions in nearby game parks. It is the de facto capital of the East African Community and hosts the International Criminal

Tribunal for Rwanda, a UN court set up to investigate and prosecute persons responsible for genocide in Rwanda in 1994.

Ash Pit: A 120-meter (400 feet) dune of volcanic ash lying at the bottom of Reutsch Crater on Kibo Peak. The ash is a remnant of the last eruption on Kilimanjaro, a now-extinct volcano.

Bagamoyo: The former capital of German East Africa from 1885 to 1890 is a historic town with some beautiful resorts on the Indian Ocean.

Barafu Huts: The base camp below the Kibo Peak summit on the Machame Route, where climbers stage for a steep, scrambling ascent to Stella Point en route to Uhuru Peak.

Breach Wall: The most difficult route to the summit with a 100-meter-high ascent up an ice wall.

Bunchgrass: A type of field grass common in the lowlands and highlands of Kilimanjaro.

Camelback hose: A drinking hose that attaches to a water bottle, allowing the bottle to be readily accessed when stored in a backpack.

Camp One: Also known as Camp First Cave, Camp One is the first campground on the Rongai Route, located about 2,700 meters (8,900 feet) above sea level. The vertical rise on the 13-kilometer (eight mile) hike from the trailhead starting at 1,800 meters (6,400 feet) is about 900 meters (3,000 feet).

Camp Two: Camp Two, also called Camp Second Cave, is the second campground on the Rongai Route, located about 3,450 meters (11,300 feet) above sea level. The vertical rise on the 12-

kilometer hike from Camp One is about 750 meters (2,500 feet). **Camp Three:** Also known as Camp Third Cave, Camp Three is located on a spur of the Rongai Route at 3,850 meters (12,650 feet) above sea level. The vertical rise on the six-kilometer hike from Camp Two is about 500 meters (1,650 feet).

Dar Es Salaam: Tanzania's largest city, commercial center, and major seaport. It is located on the Indian Ocean.

Daypack: A small, lightweight backpack designed to wear while hiking. It should be large enough to carry one or two bottles of water with extra space for food or other small items.

Dendrosenecio: A cactus-like groundsel tree with a trunk like a palm tree topped with spiky leaf rosettes. The tree is found in the highlands of Mount Kilimanjaro.

Diamox (acetazolamide): A drug taken daily in 1000 milligram doses to fend off altitude sickness (AMS).

Gaiters: Garment that resembles cowboy's chaps worn over clothing to protect legs and knees from scree, loose rock and gravel.

Gilman's Point: A transit point for most climbers on the volcanic rim of Kibo Peak at 5,585 meters (18,361 feet) A.M.S.L. Climbers ascending from Kibo Huts reach Gilman's Point before continuing to Stella Point or Uhuru Peak.

Glissade: A way to descend a steep snow- or scree-covered slope via a controlled slide on one's feet or buttocks.

Harry Street: A semi-autobiographical character in Ernest Hemingway's 1936 short story *The Snows of Kilimanjaro*. Gregory Peck played Harry in the 1952 movie of the same name.

High altitude cerebral edema (HACE): A severe, and often fatal, form of altitude sickness caused by swelling of the brain tissue. The condition occurs at altitudes above 2,500 meters (8,200 feet).

High altitude pulmonary edema (HAPE): A life-threatening condition where the lungs swell from fluid accumulation at altitudes above 2,500 meters (8,200 feet).

Horombo Huts: A camp on the Marangu Route about five hours up trail from Mandara Huts and four hours down trail from Kibo Huts.

Kibo Huts: The base camp below the Kibo Peak summit where the Marangu and Rongai routes converge. The camp is located 4,700 meters (15,400 feet) above sea level. The vertical rise on the six-kilometer hike from Camp Three on the Rongai Route is about 850 meters (2,800 feet).

Kibo Peak/Kibo Summit: The highest of the three volcanic cones on Kilimanjaro. Uhuru Peak is the highest point on Kibo Peak. Climbers on their way to the summit usually pass Gilman's Point and Stella Point, two other well-known points on the peak's rim.

Lemosho Route: A longer, lesser-used route that passes through the Shira Plateau. Climbers on this route reach the summit either via the Western Breach or Barafu Huts on the Machame Route. Lemosho offers frequent animal sightings, and guides are required to carry firearms in the event that climbers stumble upon predators.

Lobelia deckenii: A cactus-like flowering plant found in the highlands of Kilimanjaro.

Loitokitok: Small village where the Rongai Route begins.

Lusaka: The capital and largest city in Zambia where I lived from

2009 to 2011.

Malaria: A mosquito-borne infectious disease that causes fever, headaches, and in severe cases, comas or death. Malaria does not occur on Mount Kilimanjaro because it is too high for the malaria-bearing mosquitos, but cases have been reported in the lowlands in and around Arusha and Moshi. Consult your doctor prior to travel about taking malaria pills.

Mandara Huts: A camp on the Marangu Route about four hours up trail from Marangu Gate.

Marangu Gate: The park headquarters of Kilimanjaro National Park located at the trailhead of the Marangu Route. It lies about half an hour east of Moshi.

Marangu Route: Also known as the "Coca-Cola" Route, it is the most popular route on Kilimanjaro and typically takes six days to complete. Its camps have better facilities than those on other routes. The trail starts at the Marangu Gate. Some claim that it is the easiest route and has a higher success rate because it allows climbers more time to acclimatize.

Moshi: A town in the Kilimanjaro Region to the south of Mount Kilimanjaro. It is a major jumping off point for Kilimanjaro climbs and safari expeditions in nearby game parks.

Mount Kilimanjaro: A dormant volcano in Tanzania near the Kenyan border, Kilimanjaro is the highest mountain in Africa at 5,895 meters (19,341 feet) A.M.S.L. Arguably the world's highest freestanding mountain, it spreads across 3,885 square kilometers (1,500 square miles) and is capped by three volcanic cones, Kibo,

Mawenzi, and Shira. It is one of the Seven Summits, a group of the highest mountains on each of the world's seven continents.

Mount Mawenzi: The second highest of three volcanic cones on Kilimanjaro, it lies to the south of the Kibo Summit. Mawenzi is well known for its jagged, Alpine profile.

Machame Route: Also known as the "Whiskey" Route, the Machame is the shortest and steepest route to the summit. It begins on the south side of Kilimanjaro and ascends Kibo Peak via a steep scramble from Barafu Huts. The hard and fast ascent generally decreases climbers' odds of reaching the summit but may be suitable for those who adjust quickly to higher altitudes.

Mweka Route: A short, steep route used only for descent that begins at Barafu Huts and heads south. Climbers on the Machame Route often use it to descend.

Nalemuru/Nalemoru/Loitokitok/Simba Route: Other names for the new Rongai Route. The original Rongai Route began in the village of Rongai, but the trail was closed, and the Nalemuru was unofficially renamed the Rongai Route.

Ngorongoro Conservation Area: A conservation area and UNESCO World Heritage Site about 180 kilometers (110 miles) west of Kilimanjaro with thousands of game animals and exotic plant life. The caldera of an extinct volcano, it is a great destination for a safari expedition.

Northern Circuit: A lesser-used route that circles the north side of Kibo Peak. Climbers using this route must use another one to reach the summit.

Northern Icefield: Kilimanjaro's largest ice field located on the northeastern slopes of Kibo Peak.

Old man's beard: Also known as usnea lichen or tree moss, this type of lichen grows in the wet moorlands around Kilimanjaro.

Outfitter/tour operator/guide: A guide or company hired to lead your climb. You must have a licensed guide with you to climb Kilimanjaro.

Porter: Members of a support team charged with carrying gear and equipment on climbs, setting up, and tearing down camps. Porters on Kilimanjaro can legally carry up to 15 kilograms (33 pounds).

Reutsch Crater: The 2.5-kilometer-wide, deep caldera at the top of Kibo Peak, a now-extinct volcano.

Rongai Route: A moderately steep route starting on the north side of Kilimanjaro close to the Kenyan border. It usually takes six days. Some claim that it is the easiest route and has a higher success rate because it allows more time to acclimatize. The route is relatively sheltered from the elements on the drier side of the mountain, less crowded, and scenic with its alpine vistas.

School Hut: Nestled on a rock perch 4,700 meters (15,400 feet) up on the slopes of Kibo Peak, School Hut is a mountain training facility for park rangers with some campsites available on a limited basis. It is located on a spur of the Rongai Route.

Scree/talus: An accumulation of broken rock fragments at the base of crags or mountain cliffs.

Shira Peak/Plateau: The lowest of three volcanic cones on Kilimanjaro, it lies to the east of the Kibo Summit and forms the apex of the Shira Plateau.

Shira Plateau Route: A long, lesser-used route on the Shira Plateau that merges with the Lemosho Route at Shira Caves Campsite.

Stella Point: A prominent scarp on the rim of Kibo Peak located between Gilman's Point and Uhuru Peak. It rises 5,695 meters (18,681 feet) A.M.S.L.

The Saddle: A large, desolate mountain plateau between Kibo Peak and Mount Mawenzi. The Marangu Route cuts through The Saddle between Kibo Huts and Horombo Huts.

Uhuru Peak: The highest point on Kibo Peak and the summit of Mount Kilimanjaro at 5,895 meters (19,341 feet) A.M.S.L. Uhuru Peak is a relatively flat scarp on the volcanic rim of Kibo Peak. The highest point is marked by a summit sign posted by the Tanzanian government.

Umbwe Route: Also known as the "Vodka" Route, it is one of the most difficult routes on Kilimanjaro. Climbers usually ascend Kibo Summit via the Western Breach. It requires some technical skill, a high level of endurance, and an increased tolerance for high altitudes. It is prone to rockslides and sometimes icy, requiring climbers to cut ice steps or wear crampons.

Western Breach/Arrow Glacier Route: A scrambling ascent to the Kibo summit on the Lemosho Route considered the second most difficult on Kilimanjaro. It was closed in 2006 when a rockslide killed several climbers but reopened in December 2007.

Zambia: A country in southern Africa southeast of Tanzania and my former home.

Zanzibar: A semi-autonomous part of Tanzania made up of an archipelago of islands in the Indian Ocean not far from Dar Es Salaam. It is a major tourist destination in Tanzania.

21. Gearing Up for the Climb

The following is a list of items you may want to bring on your climb. Not all the items on this list may be necessary. Use your judgment and consult your guide if you have questions about what to pack.

Clothing

In general, choose synthetic knits, fleece, and other fabrics that insulate the body and are rain resistant. Quantities depend on how long your climb will be. In most cases, one of each is fine. Some clothing and undergarments like underwear, socks, and long underwear should be changed more frequently.

- Shirts (long-sleeve and synthetic)
- T-shirts (short-sleeve and synthetic)
- Hiking shorts (synthetic)
- Underwear
- Long or thermal underwear/trousers/long johns (light and synthetic)
- Socks/sock liners (light and synthetic)
- Heavy socks (wool or synthetic blend)
- Thin hiking pants
- Thick hiking pants
- Waterproof pants (breathable)
- Waterproof jacket (breathable)
- Rain poncho
- Sweater (fleece or down)
- Light jacket (fleece or down)

- Leg gaiters
- Fleece glove liners
- Light gloves
- Heavy gloves
- Bandana/head scarf
- Sun hat/floppy hat/baseball cap
- Warm/winter hat
- Balaclava/face mask
- Hiking boots (medium weight and water proof)
- Walking/tennis shoes (some traction)
- Sandals (camp)
- Sunglasses (Alpine and UV-resistant with side gussets)

Equipment

- Soft duffel bag or backpack (waterproof and portable for porters will carry)
- Daypack (large and durable)
- Mountain sleeping bag (rated ten degree Fahrenheit or warmer for cold weather)
- Mattress pad (thin and durable)
- Plastic bags of different sizes (to protect clothes against rain)
- Hiking poles
- Headlamp (with extra batteries and light bulb)
- Extra warm blanket
- Pocket knife
- Three one-liter water bottles or substitute with a hydration pack
- Water bottles (two large and able to carry 2-3 liters; camelback hose optional)
- Pocket knife/multi-tool knife

First Aid and Medications

Your first-aid kit should include the following:

- Water purification tablets
- Blister patches / mole-skin
- Adhesive bandages
- Antiseptic/antibacterial ointment or cream
- Elastic support bandage (ace-wrap)
- Safety pins
- Nail scissors
- Tweezers
- Sunscreen/sun block (rated at least 70 sun protection factor/SPF or higher)
- Insect repellent
- Hand sanitizer or handi-wipes
- Eye drops
- Lip balm
- Analgesics/pain killers, including Tylenol (acetaminophen), aspirin, ibuprofen, heat rub for sore muscles
- Stomach medicine/anti-acid
- Throat lozenges
- Prescription medicines

Consult your doctor regarding any medications you may need, including Diamox (Acetazolamide), to prevent altitude sickness.

Food

- Energy drink mix (for energy and to mask taste of boiled water)
- Energy snacks (granola bars, power bars, nuts, dried meat)
- Comfort food (chocolate, candy, Pop-Tarts)

Personal items

- Towel
- Wash cloth
- Soap
- Shampoo (travel size)
- Toothbrush
- Toothpaste
- Toilet paper
- Digital camera and extra battery
- Music player
- Reading material or e-reader
- Notebook and pen
- Extra batteries (for electronic devices)
- Travel binoculars
- Passport
- Tanzanian Visa
- Cash (U.S. dollars or Tanzanian schillings) and/or traveler's cheques
- Visa credit card (required to pay the US$800 park entrance fee as of 2011)

22. Getting By In Swahili

A little Swahili can go a long way. Knowing a few phrases of the primary language of Tanzania can make all the difference in the world in your moment of need on Mount Kilimanjaro. Below are lists of some more common words and phrases you may want to learn before your climb. Swahili spellings are generally phonetic and pronounced as they are written.

Basic Phrases

Please bring me a blanket: Ulete blanketi tafadhali
Please bring me hot water: Lete maji moto tafadhali
Can you help me: Tafadhali or naomba msaada
Do you speak English: Unasema Kiingereza
Do you speak Swahili: Unasema Kiswahili
Do you have a map: Unayo ramani
Excuse me: Samahani
Fine (in response): Nzuri
Good morning: Habari za asubuhi
Good afternoon: Habari za mchana
Goodbye: Kwa heri (one person) or Kwa herini (more than one person)
Good night: Usiku mwema or lala salama
Hello: Jambo (better to say "hujambo" when saying hello and "sijambo" when responding) or salama
How are you: Habari gani
How do you say…in Swahili: Unasemaje…kwa Kiswahili
How far is it: Jinsi mbali ni
How much: Kiasi gani

I don't understand: Sielewi
I am cold: Mimi ni baridi
I am from…: Natokea…
I am lost: Mimi waliopotea
I am sick: Mimi ni mgonjwa
I am thirsty: Nina kiu
I am tired: Mimi nimechoka
I feel better: Mimi kujisikia vizuri
I have a headache: Nina maumivu ya kichwa
I need a doctor: Nataka kuona daktari
I want to go down: Nataka kwenda chini
It hurts here: Naumwa hapa
I would like: Nataka...
A little bit: Kidogo tu
May I take your picture: Naomba kupiga picha
Much more comfortable: Afadhali sana
My name is…: Jina langu ni…
Okay: Sawa
Nice to meet you: Nafurahi kukuona
No: Hapana
Please: Tafadhali
See you later: Baadaye or Tutaonana
Slow / slowly: Pole pole
Stop: Simama
Thank you / thank you very much: Asante / asante sana
There's been an accident: Kumekuwa na ajali
Wait / wait here: Ngoja / ngoja hapa
Welcome / please come in: Karibu
What does it cost: Shilingi Ngapi
What is your name: Jina lako nani
Where are you from: Unatoka wapi

Where are we: Sisi tupa wapi
Where can I find a...: Naweza kupata...wapi
Where is...: Iko wapi...
You're welcome: Starehe
Yes: Ndiyo

Useful Words

Beer: Bia
Cold: Baridi
Doctor: Daktari or mganga
Friend: Rafiki
Guide: Kuongoza
Diarrhea: Kuhara, harisha, or endesha
Drinking water: Maji ya kunywa
Fever: Homa
Food: Chakula
Headache: Umwa kichwa
Hospital / medical center: Hospitali / matibabu
Hot: Ya moto
Hot water: Maji ya moto
Madam / Ms.: Bibi
Malaria: Melaria
Meat: Nyama
Medicine: Dawa
Mister / sir: Bwana
Nausea: Kichefuchefu
Park ranger: Hifadhi ya mgambo
Porter: Mpagazi
Rope: Kamba
Soda (soft drink): Soda

Toilet paper: Karatasi ya choo

Vegetables: Mboga

Vomiting: Kutapika

Water: Maji

Time, Distance and Direction

Hour: Saa

Go straight: Kwenda moja kwa moja

Left: Kushoto

Meter: Mita

Minute: Dakika

Right (turn): Kulia

Today: Leo

Tomorrow: Kesho

Tonight: Leo usiku

Yesterday: Jana

Now: Sasa

Later: Baadaye

Every day: Kila siku

Days of the Week

Monday: Jumatatu

Tuesday: Jumanne

Wednesday: Jumatano

Thursday: Alhamisi

Friday: Ijumaa

Saturday: Jumamosi

Sunday: Jumapili

Numbers

1: Moja

2: Mbili

3: Tatu

4: Nne

5: Tano

6: Sita

7: Saba

8: Nane

9: Tisa

10: Kumi

11: Kumi na moja

12: Kumi na mbili

20: Ishirini

21: Ishirni na moja

30: Thelathini

40: Arobaini

50: Hamsini

60: Sitini

70: Sabini

80: Themanini

90: Tisini

100: Mia

200: Mia mbili

1,000: Elfu

23. For Your Information

This book is not intended to be a full-service guide to help you climb Mount Kilimanjaro. To learn more about the mountain, hiring a guide, preparing to climb, and other information you need to know to climb Kilimanjaro, visit these helpful resources:

Climb Mount Kilimanjaro
http://www.climbmountkilimanjaro.com/

Climbing Kilimanjaro
http://www.climbingkilimanjaro.com.au/

Kili Adventures
http://www.kiliadventures.com/

Kilimanjaro Travel Guide
http://kilimanjarotravelguide.com/

Kilimanjaro Travel Adventures
http://www.kilimanjaro.com/

Mt. Kilimanjarologue
http://www.mtkilimanjarologue.com/

Seven Summits
http://7summits.com/kilimanjaro/kilimanjaro-books.php

World Adventurers
http://worldadventurers.wordpress.com/

Preview of Eurasia

Book Two in the World Adventurers Series

Enjoy this preview of "Eurasia: A Poor Student's Trek through Europe and Asia," the second book in the World Adventurers Series. The book will chronicle the author's adventures when he spent six months as a college student visiting 19 countries in Europe, the Russian Federation, and the People's Republic of China. Coming in 2012.

My arrival in Frankfurt, Germany took a turn for the worse when my fragile luggage carrier broke as I tried to pull it into the elevator, spilling my bags on the floor. Embarrassed, I abandoned the elevator to reclaim my luggage. I groaned and pulled them out of the elevator's path. I squatted next to the pile that had once been my carefully crafted plan and set my most important possessions — my passport, train ticket, traveler's checks, and plane ticket — on the floor while I lamented over what to do. In my distress, I forgot that I brought along a fanny pack to secure my valuables. The carrier lay in a twisted heap at my feet.

Suddenly, I had to figure out how to transport two large suitcases, a duffle bag and shoulder bag — virtually my entire life — hundreds of kilometers to Austria. I wished I had listened to others' sage advice to travel light, but I dismissed it because I thought I needed to over pack to survive six months on the road. I could have done without so much stuff. I thought about using an airport baggage cart, but it would have only gotten me as far as the airport subway station.

"May I help you?" a voice asked me. I looked up and saw a man standing over me. He was casually dressed in a T-shirt and jeans with a small shoulder bag. I immediately answered, "Sure, thanks."

"My name is Francisco. I'm from Venezuela but live here in Frankfurt," he said, extending his hand. I shook it and introduced myself. "Nice to meet you, Francisco. Thanks for your help."

Unsure whether he was trustworthy, I scooped up my papers and money and stashed them in my fanny pack. Francisco helped me drag my suitcases to a money exchange office, where I changed U.S. dollars into Deutschmark (DM), Germany's currency at the time. He waited patiently. I started to gather my belongings to drag alone to the subway until he said, "Here, I'm going to that way. I'll give you a hand."

I appreciated the help and gave him a suitcase to carry. We took the elevator down to the subway level of the airport. I bought an all-day pass for the Frankfurt subway at a kiosk. Again, Francisco waited for me. We took the train to the *Hauptbahnhof*, the city's main station. As the train barreled toward the city, the nondescript suburbs passed by in a drab blur. My companion explained that he grew up in Venezuela but came to Frankfurt to study architecture and never left. He spoke excellent English with a Spanish-laced accent. When I asked him how he learned the language, he responded that he needed it to communicate with people from around the world.

I started to warm up to Francisco but was still on guard for suspicious activity. Something bothered me about him. Perhaps it was that he was willing to go beyond the call of duty to help a stranger for seemingly nothing in return. I heard stories of tourists who fell victim to scams — or worse. His story seemed credible enough, and I figured that I was relatively safe accompanying him in a high-traffic area of a low-crime city. He explained that he was on his way home when he saw me. He was heading to the *Hauptbahnhof* anyway to take a train home and did not mind going with me.

When we disembarked from the subway at the main train station, Francisco happened to meet his friend Thomas, a German man with unkempt blond hair dressed in fatigues. This was odd. Thomas had a look in his eye that told me he was a streetwise sort. The fatigues made him look as if he was ready for jungle warfare, odd attire to wear in a large European city. I wanted to trust these would-be Good Samaritans, but I could not help but being suspicious of my new acquaintances or get past the nagging feeling that I was being set up. Francisco had one of my suitcases. I had to find a way to get it back and say goodbye before they separated me from my luggage — or worse.

I asked Francisco where I could find a locker, hinting that I would go alone. My apprehension turned to distrust when he said, "You have to be careful here, man. The train station is in a bad area of town where a lot of people get robbed. We can help you out."

Alarm bells went off in my head. I needed to get my belongings back and bid them goodbye as delicately as I could, fast.

About the Author

Michael Gene (M.G.) Edwards is a writer of books and stories in the mystery, thriller and science fiction-fantasy genres. He also writes travel adventures. He graduated from the University of Washington with a master's degree in China Studies and a Master of Business Administration. A former U.S. diplomat, he served in South Korea, Paraguay, and Zambia before leaving the Foreign Service in 2011 to write full time. He lives in Bangkok, Thailand with his wife Jing and son Alex.

To read more books and stories by M.G. Edwards, visit www.mgedwards.com.

Books by M.G. Edwards

Fiction

Alexander the Salamander

Real Dreams: Thirty Years of Short Stories

World Adventurers Series

Kilimanjaro: One Man's Quest to Go Over the Hill

Eurasia: A Poor Student's Trek through Europe and Asia
(Coming in 2012)

Printed in Great Britain
by Amazon.co.uk, Ltd.,
Marston Gate.